# STORM RIDERS
## by Wing Shing Ma

**Author**
Wing Shing Ma

**Translator**
Derek Wong

**Editors**
Shawn Sanders
Kevin P. Croall
Angel Cheng
Duncan Cameron

**Production Artist**
Hung-Ya Lin

**US Cover Design**
Hung-Ya Lin

**Production Manager**
Janice Chang

**Art Director**
Yuki Chung

**Marketing**
Nicole Curry

**President**
Robin Kuo

www.comicsworld.com

**English translation by**
ComicsOne Corporation 2003

**Publisher**
ComicsOne Corp.
48531 Warm Springs Blvd., Suite 408
Fremont, CA 94539
www.ComicsOne.com

**First Edition: March 2004**
ISBN 1-58899-361-2

Ⓐ *The "chess form" head figure is mark of and used under
license from Magnum Consultants Limited.*

**Relationship Chart**

Exceptionally powerful martial artist with plans of controlling the World Fighting Association. He takes on Wind and Cloud as his disciples in order to fulfill half of his destiny. The other half reveals that Wind and Cloud, his greatest assets will be the instruments of his demise. In defiance Conquer sows seeds of discord between the two pupils, hoping they will destroy each other. If not then he is determined to do it personally. After 100 years, the famous weapons clan – Sword Worship Villa is on the cusp of completing Ultimate Sword. It is there where Conquer plans to first extinguish Cloud.
**Technique**: Chi of Triplication Returns to One, Triplication Fingers

## Conquer

*Ally of Conquer*

For over a decade Wong Tong lead a faction of 108 merciless assassins collectively known as the Heavenly Pool. However, the people of the country called on the mighty Sword Saint to confront the guild. He smashed the Heavenly Pool after a vicious battle, reducing their number to a mere 12. These "Deadly Twelve" joined Conquer and helped him establish his Conquer Clan. Once the clan was in place they retired to "Highest Chamber", and planned to stay for the rest of their days. But the chamber has been destroyed…
**Technique**: The mysterious youth scroll

## Wong Tong

*Three Disciples of Conquer*

This was Conquer's 2nd in command. He held his elite status until he discovered Conquer's plot to destroy Wind and Cloud which inadvertently led to the death of his wife Kong-Chi at the hands of Cloud himself. Frost tried to rally several sympathizers who shared his averse for Conquer, including Wind and Cloud. A great battle ensued and Frost lost both his arms to save the downtrodden pupils.
**Technique**: Sky Frost Fist

## Frost

The stoic, solitary son of swordsman Master Ho and former Leader of The World Fighting Association's Cloud Corps is but another pawn in Conquer's grand scheme. Conquer knew of Cloud's love for his adopted daughter Kong-Chi. With this knowledge he wed Kong-Chi to Clouds senior clan brother Frost. His sinister intent was to tear a rift in the relationship between the two proud men, which seemed to work perfectly. But when Wen Motley explained Conquer's destiny foretold by Mud Buddha, in the minds of Wind, Cloud and Frost Conquer's plot was revealed. Cloud is determined to work alone and seeks Sword Worship Villa's Ultimate Sword to exact his revenge.
**Technique**: Repelling Palm
**Weapon**: Ultimate Sword (briefly, Unrivaled Sword)

## Cloud
### (Bu-Jing-Yun)

He is the former leader for The World Fighting Association's Wind Corps and has been Conquer's trusted pupil from a very young age. Conquer knew that Kong-Chi cared little for Frost and Cloud. Her true love was Wind. Yet Conquer forced the hapless Kong-Chi to marry Frost and engage in an affair with Cloud there by sowing decent and hatred among the three clan brothers. However upon hearing the truth in the prophecy from Mud Buddha Wind decides to join Frost and Cloud in an attempt to crush Conquer. After the battle that cripples Frost, and nearly blinds Wind, he is betrayed by his old friend Duan Lang and left to die in Le Shan cave - the home of the dreaded Flame Kylin beast. Yet miraculously he appears at Sword Worship Villa just in time to save Cloud.
**Techniques**: Ice Heart Knack, Deity of Wind Kick
**Weapon**: Inherits the Snowy Saber

## Wind
### (Nie-Fong)

*Rivals*

*Rivals*

*Former Friends*

## Sword Needy

He is a master of several techniques from so many different premium sword styles that it has left him with a muddled and impure kung fu form. His real Name is "Sword Greedy." Yet he is a master swordsman in constant pursuit of the perfect blade so "Greedy" became "Needy!" Yet his greed and need for Sword Worship Villa's Ultimate Sword nearly kills him.
**Technique**: Sword Vision

*Kung Fu Brother*

## Nameless

Nameless was once the undisputed master of the Kung Fu World, having defeated his greatest rival - the legendary Sword Saint. Nameless was said to have died of grief at age 23, after his enemies poisoned his wife. Truthfully, Nameless still lives. Retired from the world of kung fu he has passed on his unmatched Nameless Sword Skill and Hero sword to his lone disciple Jien-Chen. However with the birth of the ominous Ultimate Sword the time quickly approaches for the nameless one to emerge from his retirement.
**Technique**: Nameless Sword Skill
**Weapon**: Hero Sword

## Duan-Lang

The Son of Master Duan has come a long way since his exile from the World Fighting Association. He has recently reclaimed his family heirloom - the Flame Kylin Sword! Upon finding it, he discovers its dark secret and the three-way connection between his ancestors, the sword and the Flame Kylin itself!
**Technique**: Duan Technique
**Weapon**: Inherits the Flame Kylin Sword

*Disciple of Nameless*

## Jien-Chen

This is the only pupil of Nameless. His skill in kung fu is even more than the late Sword Saint could handle! Recently in a battle at Sword Worship Villa, Jien-Chen fought to assist Cloud in his fight with the maniacal Duan Lang and his Flame Kylin sword. As Flame Kylin Sword and Jien-Chen's Hero sword clashed, the Hero Sword was snapped in two, shocking everyone present.
**Technique**: Nameless Sword Skill
**Weapon**: Inherits the Hero Sword

This giant demon of a man has reached the dark level of "Demon Sword!" Can this compare with "Flying God" or "Heaven Sword?" A powerful player, Sword Demon is only moved by one thing…Love for Sword Worship Villa's Madam Au. To win her heart he has devoted his life to helping the Villa forge the Ultimate Sword.
**Technique**: Breaking Sword Skill

## Sword Demon

# CHAPTER 56 : SWORD'S PRESENCE, CLOUD'S PRESENCE

HOW FAR UNTIL WE REACH THE VILLAGE OF PARADISE?

NOT FAR AT ALL! IT'S AT THE END OF THIS RIVER

ISN'T THIS PLACE BEAUTIFUL? IT WOULD BE WONDERFUL TO LIVE HERE.

WIND AND CLOUD HAVE BEEN SEPARATED SINCE LIN-YIN CAVE.

CLOUD ACCOMPANIES CHU-CHU ON HER WAY TO VISIT JIEN-CHEN.

JIEN-CHEN WILL BE SURPRISED WHEN HE SEES US. HE STILL HAS TO TAKE US SIGHT-SEE-ING TOO!

JIEN-CHEN HAS A KIND PERSONALITY AND HE'S A GREAT MARTIAL ARTIST. HIS MASTER IS A WELL-KNOWN LEGEND TOO... CLOUD, YOU SHOULD TALK TO HIM MORE!

4

I WONDER WHERE FROST AND WIND ARE. WHY DIDN'T YOU THREE STAY TOGETHER FOR A FEW MORE DAYS?

CLOUD DOESN'T SAY A WORD, ENCOURAGING CHU-CHU TO GROW USED TO ANSWERING HER OWN QUESTIONS.

FINALLY HE SPEAKS!

JIEN-CHEN IS A GREAT MARTIAL ARTIST AND HE HAS ALREADY TAKEN GOOD CARE OF YOU!

NO WAY! HOW HAS HE TREATED ME ANY BETTER THAN YOU?

I PROMISED YOUR DAD I WOULD TAKE CARE OF YOU, BUT I WOULD FEEL MORE AT EASE IF I LET JIEN-CHEN LOOK AFTER YOU!

HUH? WHAT DO YOU MEAN?

I HAVE SOMETHING TO TAKE CARE OF. STAY AT JIEN-CHEN'S FOR A FEW DAYS AND I'LL FIND YOU THERE!

CLOUD!

WHERE ARE YOU GOING?

WAH! WHAT ARE YOU DOING?

KYAH!

AS CLOUD SADDLES THE HORSE, HIS POWERS FLOW THROUGH -- AWAKENING ITS SPIRIT!

YAH!

WITH CLOUD'S CRY, THE HORSE CHARGES OFF WITH NEWFOUND VIGOR!

I'M LOOKING FOR JIEN-CHEN, IS HE AROUND?

YEAH! HOLD ON, I'LL GET HIM FOR YOU!

YOUNG MASTER! THERE'S A BEAUTIFUL GIRL LOOKING FOR YOU!

STOP KIDDING AROUND, FAIRY MAN!

OH, CHU-CHU!

ONCE JIEN-CHEN SEES CHU-CHU, A LIGHT BASHFUL SMILE APPEARS ON HIS FACE.

JIEN-CHEN, AM I GLAD TO SEE YOU!

IS THERE SOMETHING WRONG? DON'T WORRY, YOU CAN TALK TO ME!

CHU-CHU SLOWLY EXPLAINS THE SITUATION TO JIEN-CHEN.

HE UNDERSTANDS AND COMFORTS THE YOUNG WOMAN.

WORRY NOT, CLOUD IS VERY SKILLED. WHY DON'T YOU STAY HERE FOR A FEW DAYS AND WAIT FOR HIM!

JIEN-CHEN, I HAVE A FAVOR TO ASK OF YOU, WILL YOU DO IT?

DON'T BE AFRAID, I'LL TRY MY BEST TO HELP YOU!

JIEN-CHEN HAS HAD A CRUSH ON CHU-CHU FROM THE BEGINNING AND AGREES TO HER REQUEST WITHOUT HESITATION.

I KNOW CLOUD'S PERSONALITY... WITH CONQUER INJURED, CLOUD WILL GO AFTER HIM FOR SURE. WILL YOU GO WITH ME TO FIND HIM?

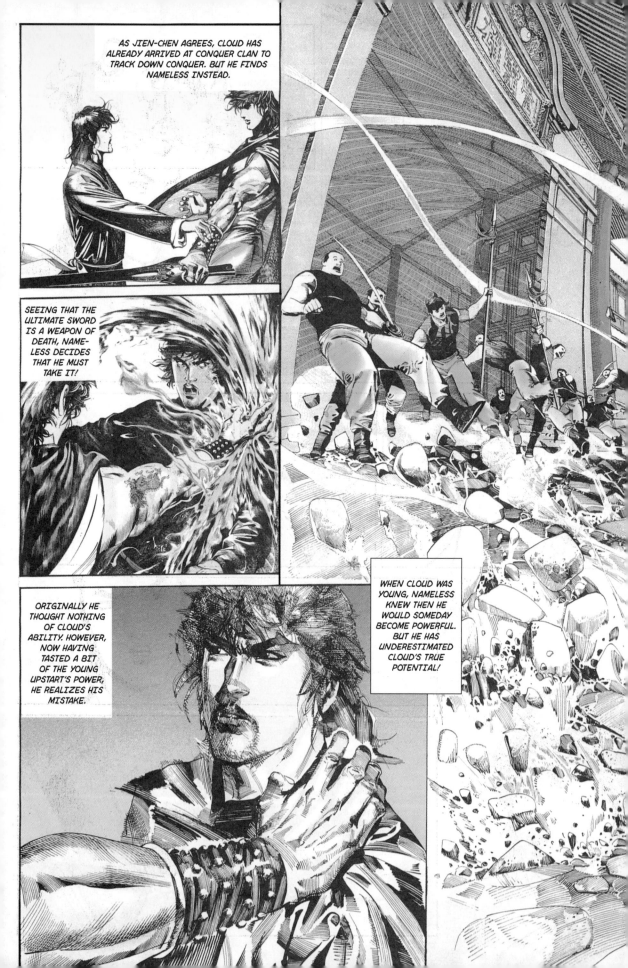

AS JIEN-CHEN AGREES, CLOUD HAS ALREADY ARRIVED AT CONQUER CLAN TO TRACK DOWN CONQUER. BUT HE FINDS NAMELESS INSTEAD.

SEEING THAT THE ULTIMATE SWORD IS A WEAPON OF DEATH, NAMELESS DECIDES THAT HE MUST TAKE IT!

ORIGINALLY HE THOUGHT NOTHING OF CLOUD'S ABILITY. HOWEVER, NOW HAVING TASTED A BIT OF THE YOUNG UPSTART'S POWER, HE REALIZES HIS MISTAKE.

WHEN CLOUD WAS YOUNG, NAMELESS KNEW THEN HE WOULD SOMEDAY BECOME POWERFUL. BUT HE HAS UNDERESTIMATED CLOUD'S TRUE POTENTIAL!

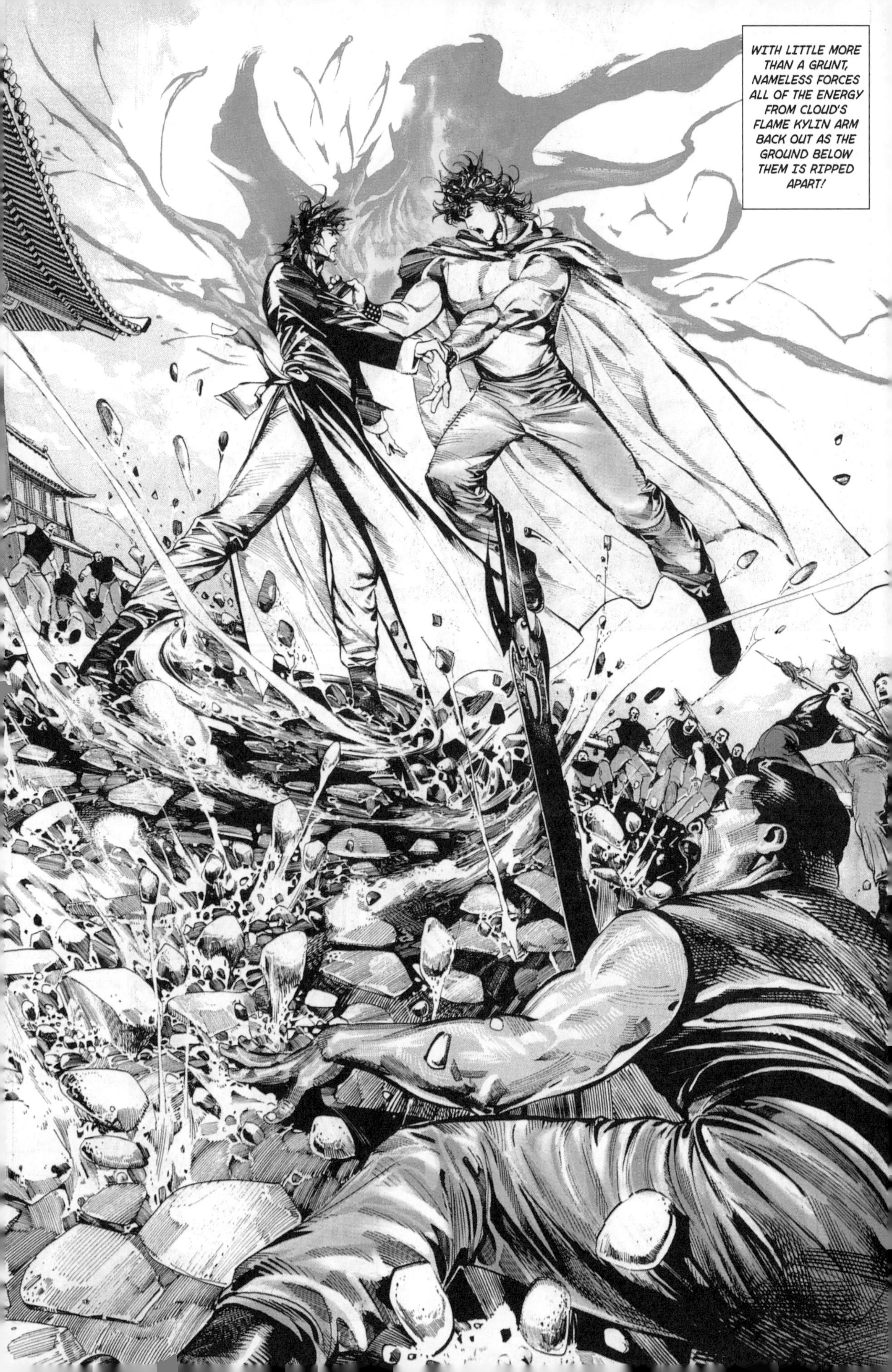
WITH LITTLE MORE THAN A GRUNT, NAMELESS FORCES ALL OF THE ENERGY FROM CLOUD'S FLAME KYLIN ARM BACK OUT AS THE GROUND BELOW THEM IS RIPPED APART!

SKILLFULLY THE LEGENDARY FIGHTER DIRECTS THE ENERGY TOWARD THE NEARBY WELL, EVAPORATING ITS WATER.

NAMELESS GRUNTS ONCE MORE AS CLOUD IS PUSHED AWAY!

BEFORE RECEIVING HIS FLAME KYLIN ARM, CLOUD WAS EASILY DEFEATED BY SWORD SAINT!

EVEN WITH HIS NEW ABILITIES, NAMELESS CAN STILL PUSH CLOUD BACK WITHOUT MOVING AN INCH.

ODDLY, NOW THE ULTIMATE SWORD BEGINS TO MOVE.

HAH.

NAMELESS NEVER MEANT TO HURT CLOUD, BUT STILL, BECAUSE OF HIS ROBUST CHI, CLOUD IS SENT CAREENING INTO THE NEARBY BUILDING.

WHEN CLOUD HITS THE GROUND, THE ULTIMATE SWORD FOLLOWS -- FALLING INTO HIS HAND!

SWORD WITH HEART, HEART WITH BEHAVIOR. TO BE RIGHTEOUS, THE SWORD IS RIGHTEOUS! TO BE EVIL, THE SWORD IS EVIL!

TOO POWERFUL...! JUST WASTING MY TIME...!

BOOM

CLOUD DOESN'T WANT TO FIGHT AND FLEES THROUGH THE WALL.

HE LEAVES "CONQUER COURT" AND HEADS TOWARD "FROST COURT!"

NAMELESS REMAINS STILL AS HE WATCHES CLOUD LEAVE!

IF CLOUD CONTINUES TO KILL WITHOUT PURPOSE AND BECOMES TRULY EVIL, THEN THE ULTIMATE SWORD WILL TURN INTO THE ULTIMATE SWORD OF EVIL. AT THAT POINT, NOT EVEN I WILL BE ABLE TO STOP IT. I MUST TAKE THE SWORD FROM HIM NOW!

NAMELESS IS DEEP IN THOUGHT, AS THE PEOPLE AROUND HIM DON'T DARE MAKE ANY SUDDEN MOVES.

EXCUSE ME, WHERE'S THE FROST COURT? CAN YOU BRING ME THERE?

OH! FROST COURT...

I CAN'T TAKE YOU TH...!

WITHOUT FINISHING, THE SOLDIER IS CARRIED SKYWARD.

WAHHH!

AH!

FROST COURT

CLOUD BREAKS INTO FROST COURT.

THEREIN CLOUD FINDS YORUO.

12

SHE IS BOUND TO A CHAIR WITH A MYSTERIOUS FIGURE SITTING BEHIND HER.

THIS MAN WITH THE MUSCULAR BUILD IS — MASTER "STEEL BO".

HMM... EVEN YORUO IS BEING HELD CAPTIVE. HE REALLY ISN'T HERE!

WHO ARE YOU?

I'M HERE HOLDING CONQUER'S DAUGHTER AS ORDERED BY WONG TONG!

ARE YOU CONQUER'S HENCHMAN?

I AM CON-QUER'S ENEMY!

I DON'T KNOW WHAT YOUR QUARREL WITH CONQUER IS, BUT TREATING AN INNOCENT YOUNG GIRL LIKE THIS IS WRONG.... LET HER GO!

WE'LL HAVE TO SEE WHAT YOU CAN DO IF YOU WANT TO RESCUE HER!

CLOUD'S ENEMY IS CONQUER, NOT HIS DAUGHTER. SO HE DOES NOT WANT ANY HARM TO COME TO HER.

NO...

OK! YOU'RE ASKING FOR IT!

13

AS HE STEPS IN, THE GROUND RUMBLES AND SHIFTS DOWN... A TRAP!

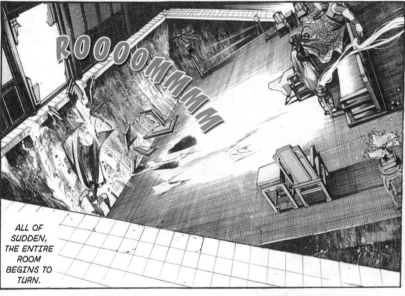

ROOOOMMMM

ALL OF SUDDEN, THE ENTIRE ROOM BEGINS TO TURN.

AT THE BOTTOM OF THE TRAP ARE HUNDREDS OF VENOMOUS SNAKES!

HISSSSS

CLOUD REMAINS CALM AS HE CRUSHES SEVERAL SNAKES WITH HIS FEET!

WITH A SWING OF THE ULTIMATE SWORD, SEVERAL OTHER SNAKES DIE AS WELL!

HAH!

BOTH MAN AND SWORD SEND OUT A SURGE OF ENERGY, AS THE SNAKES MOVE BACK!

HAHA... ISN'T MY TRAP IMPRESSIVE? LOOKS LIKE YOU AREN'T BAD YOURSELF!

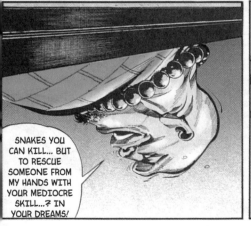

SNAKES YOU CAN KILL... BUT TO RESCUE SOMEONE FROM MY HANDS WITH YOUR MEDIOCRE SKILL...? IN YOUR DREAMS!

TURNED UPSIDE DOWN, YORUO'S HEAD IS NOW BEING PULLED BACK BY THE ROPES. A PIERCING PAIN GRIPS HER!

HAH!

CLOUD KNOWS YORUO'S LIFE IS IN DANGER AND LEAPS TO HER AID!

15

I'LL SHOW YOU MY GOLDEN BUDDHA ARMOR SKILL, BOY!

**SKY FULL OF BUDDHA**

MASTER STEEL BO JUMPS AT CLOUD AS HIS PALMS ATTACK FROM ALL DIRECTIONS!

ATTACKS OF ILLUSION DO NOT WORK ON CLOUD AS HE PREPARES HIS SWORD!

AFTER CONTACT, CLOUD'S IN SHOCK... THE ULTIMATE SWORD SLICES THROUGH THE BRACELETS, BUT NOT MASTER STEEL BO'S ARM.

KLANK

HA! MY GOLDEN BUDDHA ARMOR NOT ONLY PROTECTS MY BODY, BUT I CAN USE MY BODY TO ATTACK!

AS HE BOASTS STEEL BO ATTEMPTS A HEAD BUTT, BUT CLOUD BLOCKS IT!

WHILE BLOCKING HIGH, CLOUD OPENS HIMSELF TO A MIDSECTION ATTACK!

THOOM

CLOUD IS NO QUITTER. WHEN THE PAIN RUSHES THROUGH HIS BODY HE IMMEDIATELY COUNTERS WITH HIS "REPELLING PALM" TO MASTER STEEL BO'S HEAD!

BAM

AH! SUCH POWER!

KRASH

THE ULTIMATE SWORD CAN'T EVEN BREAK THROUGH A SIMPLE PROTECTIVE CHI STYLE LIKE THAT? MAYBE IT'S AS GRAND CHUNG SAID -- "THE SWORD HASN'T OPENED?"

THE POWER PACKED INTO MASTER STEEL BO'S STRIKE IS TOO POWERFUL AND CLOUD IS KNOCKED OUT OF THE TRAP.

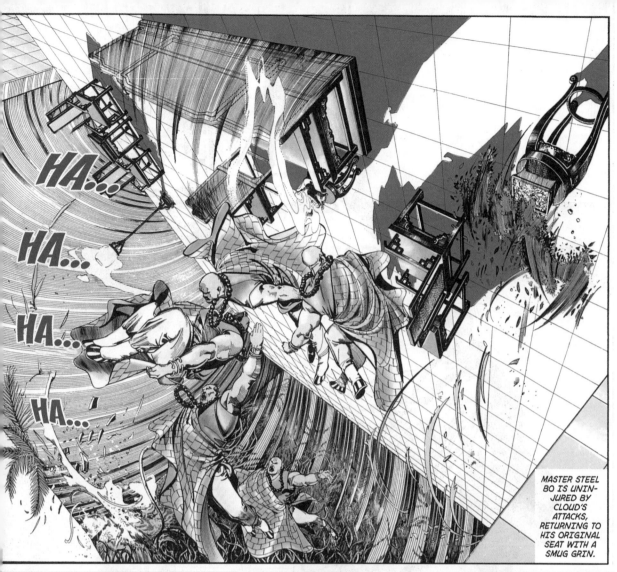

HA...

HA...

HA...

HA...

MASTER STEEL BO IS UNINJURED BY CLOUD'S ATTACKS, RETURNING TO HIS ORIGINAL SEAT WITH A SMUG GRIN.

MY GOLDEN BUDDHA ARMOR IS AT THE HIGHEST LEVEL POSSIBLE. NOT EVEN YOUR ULTIMATE SWORD CAN HARM ME. I AM INVINCIBLE!

NOT QUITE!

WHAT! HOW DARE YOU?

MASTER STEEL BO! IT WASN'T ME, IT WAS HIM!

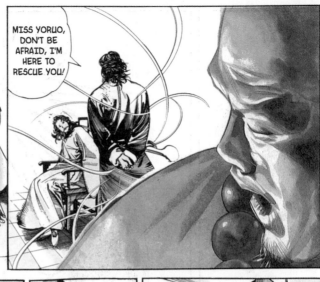

MISS YORUO, DON'T BE AFRAID, I'M HERE TO RESCUE YOU!

SHOO

THIP

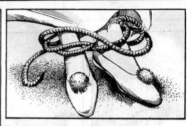

MAY I ASK WHO YOU ARE? WHY ARE YOU RESCUING ME?

*NAMELESS LIGHTLY TOUCHES YORUO. HIS UNCANNY SKILL IN INTERNAL POWER ALLOWS HIM TO RESONATE IS CHI THROUGH HER BODY. THUS NAMELESS IS ABLE TO COMMUNICATE WITH HER INTERNALLY.*

YOUR FATHER HAS ESCAPED THE GRASP OF THE DEADLY TWELVE AND IS NOW RESTING IN SAFETY.

BUT HE WAS AFRAID THAT WONG TONG WOULD STILL HARM YOU, SO HE ASKED ME TO RETRIEVE YOU.

TO ENSURE YOUR FATHER'S SAFETY ALONG WITH YOURS, PLEASE PROMISE ME YOU WON'T TALK TO ANYONE ABOUT THIS.

I... UNDER-STAND.

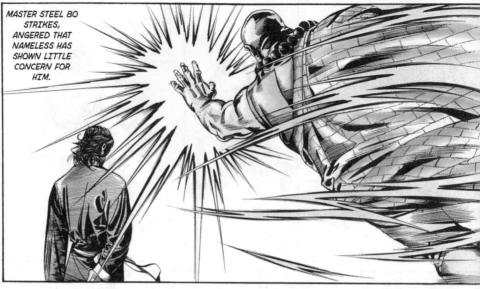

MASTER STEEL BO STRIKES, ANGERED THAT NAMELESS HAS SHOWN LITTLE CONCERN FOR HIM.

HIS ATTACK SUDDENLY STOPS.

A MERE GLANCE SHOWS NAMELESS WOULD HAVE CLAIMED HIS LIFE IF MASTER STEEL BO CONTINUED.

HE FEELS AS IF NUMEROUS INVISIBLE SWORDS NEARLY PIERCED HIS HEART.

IN SHOCK, HE RETREATS.

STEEL BO...

NAMELESS? IT'S YOU! YOU'RE ALIVE?

YOU SAID THAT YOUR GOLDEN BUDDHA ARMOR IS INVINCIBLE, WHY'D YOU RETREAT?

NAMELESS... YOU'RE NUMBER ONE ACROSS THE LANDS... I MAY HAVE CONFIDENCE IN MY GOLDEN BUDDHA ARMOR, BUT I AM NO FOOL!

AS MASTER STEEL BO FINISHES HIS WORDS, HE TRIES TO ACTIVATE THE TRAP WITH HIS FEET!

BUT NO MATTER HOW MUCH POWER HE SENDS TO THE FLOOR, NAMELESS REMAINS UNMOVED.

STEEL BO, HAVE YOU FORGOTTEN EVERYTHING THAT HAPPENED TWENTY YEARS AGO?

THEY MUST HAVE MET A LONG TIME AGO...

TWENTY YEARS AGO, AFTER NAMELESS DEFEATED THE TOP TEN CLANS OF THE LAND, NUMEROUS CHALLENGERS CAME TO HIM. HE GREW TIRED OF IT AND TRAVELED ELSEWHERE WITH HIS WIFE!

ONE DAY, THE TWO OF THEM CAME ACROSS A PEACEFUL LOOKING TEMPLE.

INSIDE THE TEMPLE, WAS A GRAND MONK... THIS MONK WAS STEEL BO.

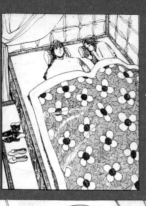

IT WAS ALREADY LATE SO NAMELESS AND HIS WIFE STAYED THE NIGHT.

THEN ALL OF A SUDDEN, THEIR BED BEGAN TO MOVE!

THEY FELL INTO A TRAP, WHICH WAS OBVIOUSLY PREPARED BEFOREHAND!

YOU'VE KILLED SO MANY TOP CLAN MEMBERS, I MUST AVENGE THEM!

THOSE CLAN MEMBERS ALL DIED FOR THE BETTER. THEY DIDN'T FIGHT RIGHTEOUSLY... I, NAMELESS, WOULD NEVER BE LIKE THEM, NOR WILL I BE LIKE YOU, USING TRAPS AND TRICKERY!

NAMELESS EASILY SLICED THROUGH THE NET!

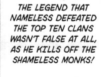

WE DON'T NEED TO FOLLOW ANY RULES AGAINST THIS KID. GET HIM!

THE LEGEND THAT NAMELESS DEFEATED THE TOP TEN CLANS WASN'T FALSE AT ALL, AS HE KILLS OFF THE SHAMELESS MONKS!

SEEING HIS COMRADES HARMED, STEEL BO ENTERS THE BATTLE, BUT NAMELESS WAS NOT ABLE TO HURT HIM!

HAHA, MY GOLDEN BUDDHA ARMOR IS ALREADY AT LEVEL SIX. YOU WON'T BE ABLE TO HURT ME AT ALL!

YOU'RE WRONG. IT'S NOT MY HERO SWORD THAT'S FIGHTING YOU, IT'S ME THAT'S FIGHTING YOU!

I MUST THINK OF A WAY TO BEAT HIM!

ALRIGHT! YOU SEEM CONFIDENT. LET US MAKE A BET!

OH?

IF YOU CAN HURT ME WITHIN TEN MOVES, I'LL PROMISE TO FOREVER STAY OUT OF YOUR WAY!

AH! YOU'RE USING THE NAME OF RIGHTEOUS-NESS TO CLAIM MY WIFE. HOW DARE YOU, YOU BASTARD!

ALRIGHT! I AGREE!

NOT SO FAST! IF YOU LOSE...

STEEL BO GIVES NAMELESS' WIFE A PERVERTED LOOK...

NAMELESS LOOKS AT HIS WIFE AND UNDER-STANDS.

IN HIS YOUTH NAMELESS WOULD EASI-LY SUCCUMB TO RAGE AND STEEL BO'S LASCIVIOUS INTENTIONS QUICKLY FUELS THE FIRE!

BLAME YOUR WIFE FOR BEING TOO BEAUTIFUL, EVEN FOR A BUDDHIST ADEPT!

AT THE SAME TIME, A HIGH PITCHED VOICE SPOKE OUT.

TEN MOVES IS TOO MUCH, MAKE IT THREE!

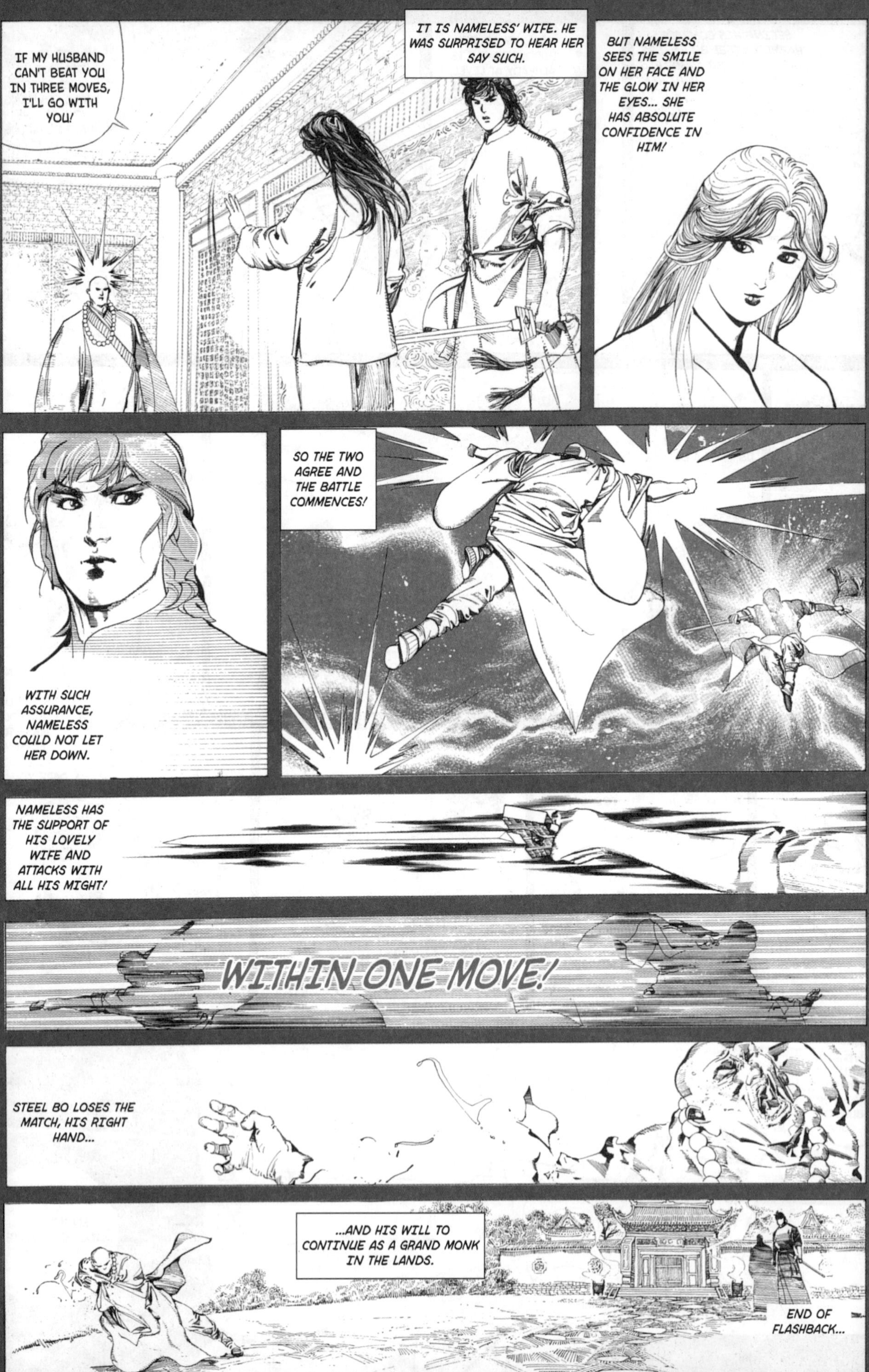
IF MY HUSBAND CAN'T BEAT YOU IN THREE MOVES, I'LL GO WITH YOU!
IT IS NAMELESS' WIFE. HE WAS SURPRISED TO HEAR HER SAY SUCH.
BUT NAMELESS SEES THE SMILE ON HER FACE AND THE GLOW IN HER EYES... SHE HAS ABSOLUTE CONFIDENCE IN HIM!
WITH SUCH ASSURANCE, NAMELESS COULD NOT LET HER DOWN.
SO THE TWO AGREE AND THE BATTLE COMMENCES!
NAMELESS HAS THE SUPPORT OF HIS LOVELY WIFE AND ATTACKS WITH ALL HIS MIGHT!
WITHIN ONE MOVE!
STEEL BO LOSES THE MATCH, HIS RIGHT HAND...
...AND HIS WILL TO CONTINUE AS A GRAND MONK IN THE LANDS.
END OF FLASHBACK...

MY GOLDEN BUDDHA ARMOR IS FAR STRONGER NOW. HOW CAN I KEEP THAT PROMISE?

NAMELESS, LET US BATTLE ONCE AGAIN!

TOO BAD I'M NOT THE SAME "NAMELESS" AS BEFORE, I DON'T WANT TO FIGHT!

NAMELESS! GET BACK HERE! WE MUST FIGHT NO MATTER WHAT!

FSHOO

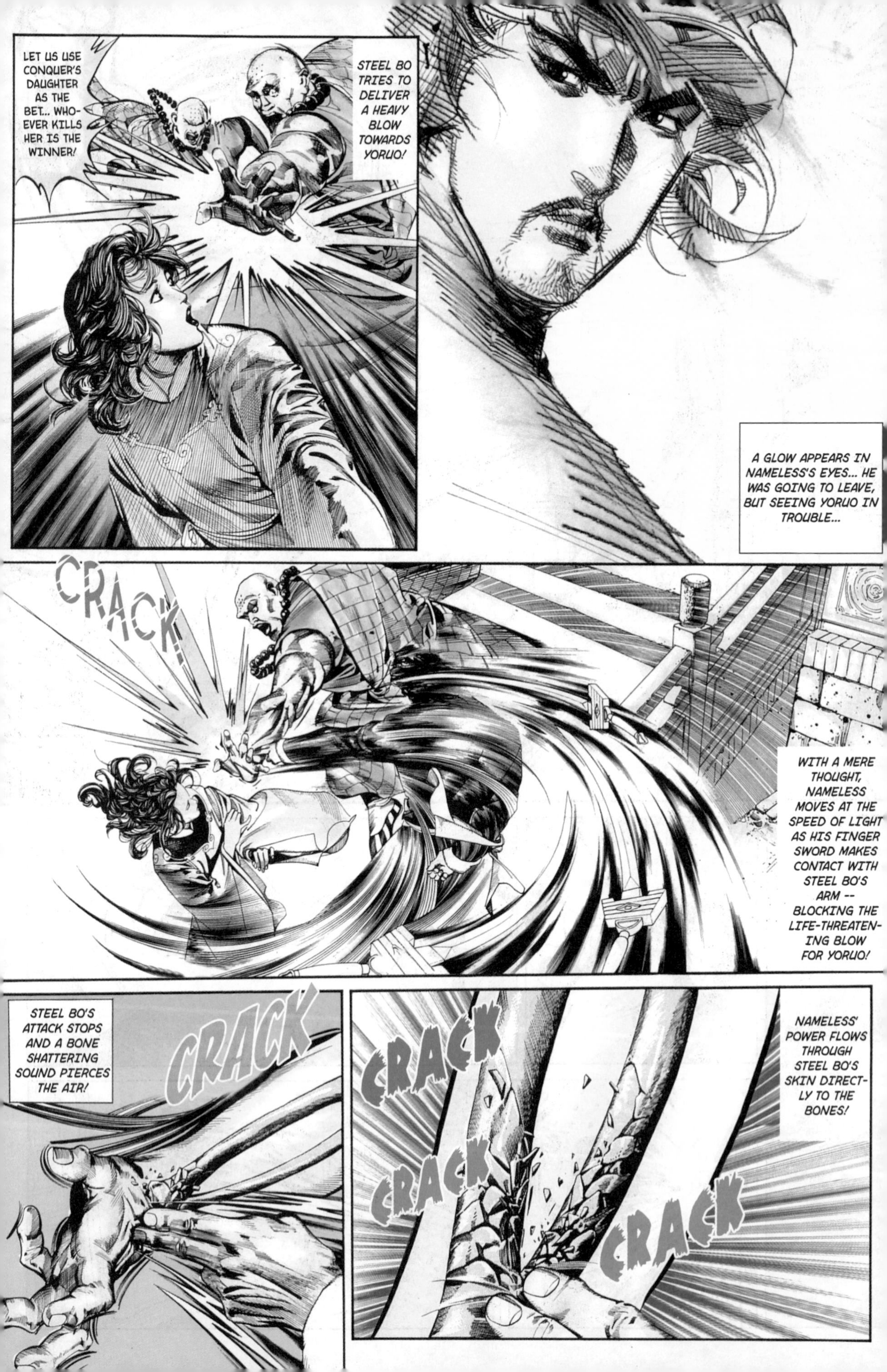

LET US USE CONQUER'S DAUGHTER AS THE BET... WHO-EVER KILLS HER IS THE WINNER!
STEEL BO TRIES TO DELIVER A HEAVY BLOW TOWARDS YORUO!
A GLOW APPEARS IN NAMELESS'S EYES... HE WAS GOING TO LEAVE, BUT SEEING YORUO IN TROUBLE...
CRACK
WITH A MERE THOUGHT, NAMELESS MOVES AT THE SPEED OF LIGHT AS HIS FINGER SWORD MAKES CONTACT WITH STEEL BO'S ARM -- BLOCKING THE LIFE-THREATEN-ING BLOW FOR YORUO!
STEEL BO'S ATTACK STOPS AND A BONE SHATTERING SOUND PIERCES THE AIR!
CRACK
NAMELESS' POWER FLOWS THROUGH STEEL BO'S SKIN DIRECT-LY TO THE BONES!
CRACK
CRACK
CRACK

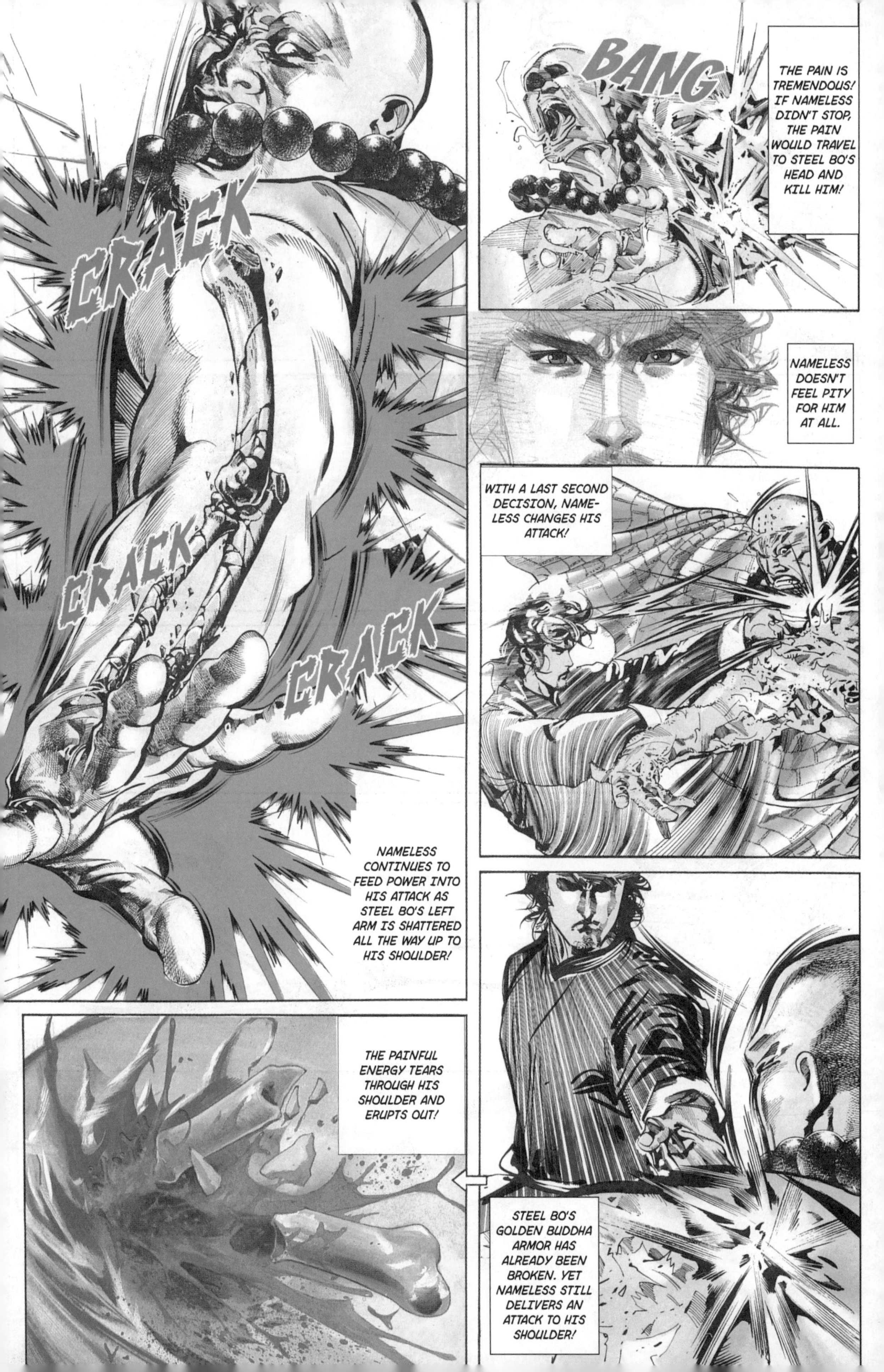
CRACK
CRACK
CRACK
NAMELESS CONTINUES TO FEED POWER INTO HIS ATTACK AS STEEL BO'S LEFT ARM IS SHATTERED ALL THE WAY UP TO HIS SHOULDER!
BANG
THE PAIN IS TREMENDOUS! IF NAMELESS DIDN'T STOP, THE PAIN WOULD TRAVEL TO STEEL BO'S HEAD AND KILL HIM!
NAMELESS DOESN'T FEEL PITY FOR HIM AT ALL.
WITH A LAST SECOND DECISION, NAME-LESS CHANGES HIS ATTACK!
STEEL BO'S GOLDEN BUDDHA ARMOR HAS ALREADY BEEN BROKEN. YET NAMELESS STILL DELIVERS AN ATTACK TO HIS SHOULDER!
THE PAINFUL ENERGY TEARS THROUGH HIS SHOULDER AND ERUPTS OUT!

HIS RIGHT ARM IS ENTIRELY USELESS AS HE CRIES IN PAIN!

YORUO'S UPBRINGING WITHIN CONQUER CLAN HAS LEFT HER UNAFFECTED BY SUCH GRUESOME BATTLES.

EVEN THOUGH YOUR GOLDEN BUDDHA ARMOR WAS INDEED POWERFUL, ANY "PROTECTION" MARTIAL ART SKILL CAN BE BROKEN. HOWEVER, YOU LOST TO ME TWENTY YEARS AGO, WHICH WAS WHY YOU HAD YOUR DOUBTS TODAY AND LOST TO ME AGAIN!

BESIDES, YOU DIDN'T KEEP YOUR "WORD"... THIS WAS YOUR DESERVED PUNISHMENT!

SIR, CLOUD ISN'T HERE ANYMORE!

NAMELESS QUICKLY TAKES YORUO AND GOES AFTER CLOUD. HE CAN'T LET HIM GET AWAY TODAY.

CLOUD IS UNABLE TO FIND CONQUER AND IS ABOUT TO DEPART.

BUT, NAMELESS IS BLOCKING HIS WAY!

CLOUD, GIVE ME THE SWORD!

THIS IS MY SWORD; I WON'T GIVE IT TO ANYONE!

IF YOU WON'T GIVE IT FREELY, THEN I'LL HAVE TO TAKE IT!

SHUT UP! SWORD'S PRESENT, CLOUD'S PRESENT! MY REVENGE ISN'T FINISHED, THE SWORD CANNOT LEAVE ME!

CLOUD CHOSE THE WRONG PATH AND DECIDES TO ATTACK NAMELESS. NOW NAMELESS IS LEFT WITH NO CHOICE.

YOU WERE ALWAYS FILLED WITH ANGER AND A HEART FOR REVENGE EVER SINCE YOU WERE A CHILD. YOU LEAVE ME NO CHOICE!

NAMELESS SWIFTLY TAKES ACTION AND STOPS THE ULTIMATE SWORD WITH HIS TWO FINGERS!

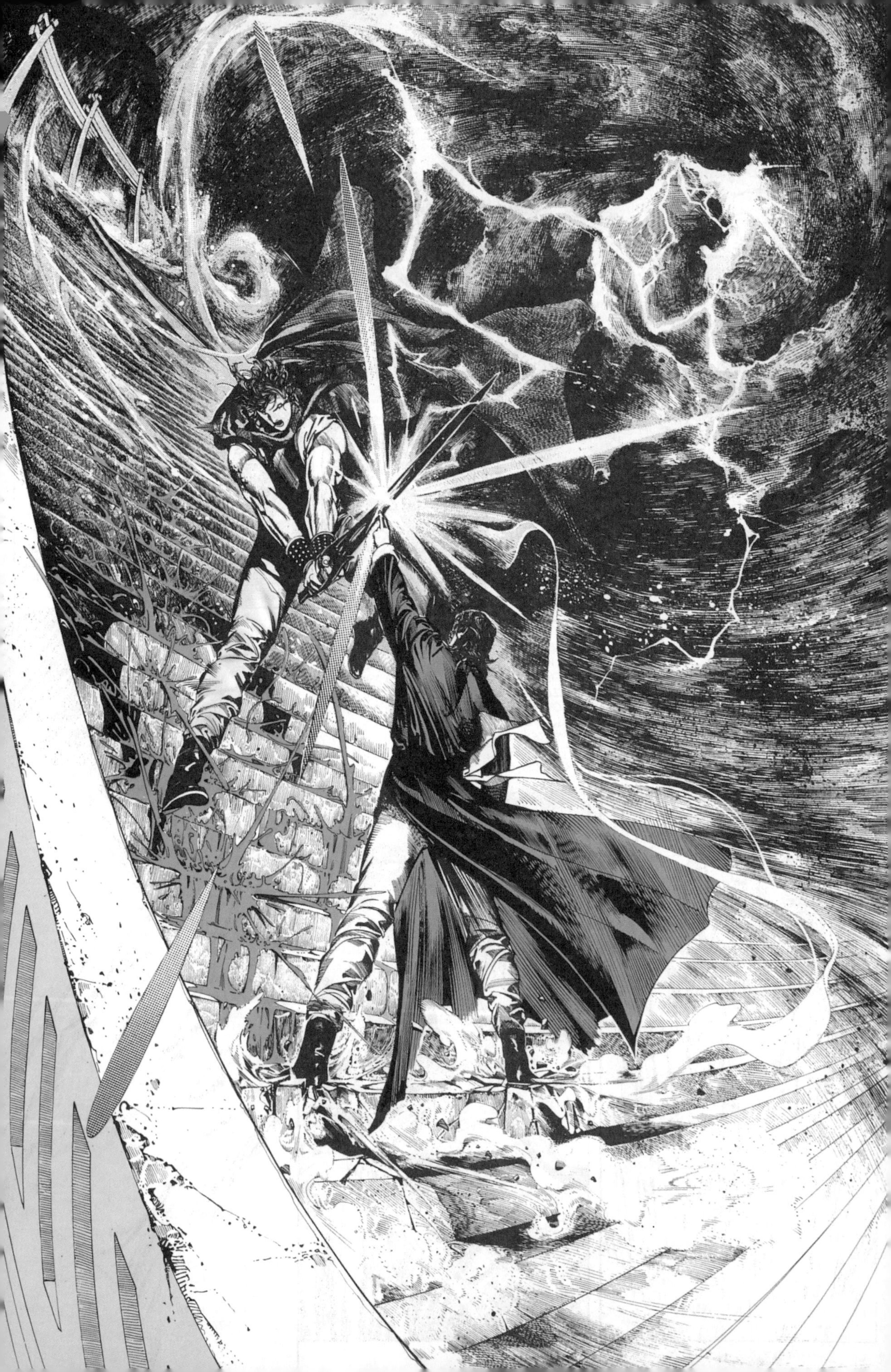

# CHAPTER 57 : WHERE DOES THE SWORD BELONG

CLOUD WOULD DIE
BEFORE PARTING WITH
HIS ULTIMATE SWORD.
AND NAMELESS WILL DO
ALL HE CAN TO RID HIM
OF IT. CLOUD VIOLENTLY
SLASHES DOWN, BUT
NAMELESS CATCHES THE
SWORD BETWEEN HIS
FINGERS...

CLOUD
CAN'T MOVE
AN INCH
FORWARD
NOR
BACKWARD!

CLOUD, LET GO
OF THE SWORD...
LET GO OF YOUR
VENGEFUL HEART.
IF YOU LET GO,
THEN YOU CAN
RID YOURSELF OF
THE EVIL!

CLOUD
IGNORES
THE MIGHTY
FIGHTER
AND ADDS
MORE POWER
TO HIS
SWORD!

LET GO!
OR ELSE
I'LL KILL
YOU!

34

NAMELESS CAN NOW FEEL CLOUD AND HIS SWORD'S URGE TO KILL... IT IS AN ENERGY THAT NAMELESS HAS NEVER FELT BEFORE. THIS IS HIS PAYMENT FOR RESCUING CLOUD AS A YOUNG BOY?

HE DECIDES TO CONFRONT IT, AS HIS EYES SHINE LIKE THE BLADE OF A SWORD!

UPON RAISING HIS INNER POWER, NUMEROUS RAYS OF LIGHT EMERGE FROM HIS BODY, RISING UPWARD!

EARLIER NAMELESS HELPED CONQUER ESCAPE THE DEADLY TWELVE WHEN HE WAS TRAINING IN THE HIDDEN LANDS. THERE, HE CREATED A NEW SWORD STYLE. UNBELIEVABLY THIS IS BEYOND HIS "NAMELESS SWORD SKILL" --

HE NAMED THE STYLE "LIMITLESS" BECAUSE THE SOURCE OF THE POWER COMES FROM THE HEART, AND IS DIVIDED INTO "SHAPELESS," "HEARTLESS," "NAMELESS," AND "SELFLESS"!

AFTER ITS CREATION, NAMELESS HAD NEVER USED IT IN AN ACTUAL FIGHT. THIS IS HIS FIRST TIME!

CLOUD CAN ONLY WATCH AS NUMEROUS SHAPELESS SWORD BEAMS RISE UP AT HIM. IT'S THE LIMITLESS SWORD SKILL'S -- SHAPELESS FORM!

LIMITLESS SWORD SKILL

VISSH

SHIK

ZING

SLSSH

35

NAMELESS USES 20% OF HIS POWER TO BREAK CLOUD'S GRIP. HE HAS NO INTENTION OF KILLING THE BRASH YOUTH!

AH, WHAT SWORD SKILL WAS THAT?

IT'S AS IF NUMEROUS SWORDS PIERCED MY BODY?!

HE DOESN'T HOLD A SWORD, BUT HIS EYES...!

THIS SWORD SKILL IS STRONGER THAN SWORD SAINT'S "SWORD SKILL 22"... IS HE HUMAN?

NO! HE'S NOT HUMAN, HE'S A "SWORD!"

RIGHT! NAMELESS IS A SWORD!

AS NAMELESS HOLDS THE ULTIMATE SWORD, IT GLOWS AS IF IT WERE JUST BORN. AS FOR NAMELESS, HE'S AN ANCIENT SWORD THAT HAS NEVER BEEN BROKEN!

THIS MAN IS TOO POWER-FUL! IT'S OBVIOUS HE COULD EASILY KILL CLOUD BUT HAS LET HIM GO SO MANY TIMES. HE MUST NOT WANT TO TAKE HIS LIFE!

TAP

TAP

TAP

AH!

YORUO KNOWS A LITTLE "DEITY OF WIND KICK" TOO, AND SHE SWIFTLY DODGES THE CHARGING MAN!

THE TWO THAT CAME RUNNING UP THE STAIRS ARE THE ULTI-MATE SWORD'S GUARDIANS -- WEN WU AND ICE!

THE TWO HAVE BEEN FOLLOWING CLOUD, DESPITE THEIR PROMISE. SEEING THAT THE SWORD HAS BEEN STOLEN, THEY ARE COM-PELLED TO HELP CLOUD RETRIEVE IT!

NAMELESS DOESN'T PANIC AT ALL AS HE SLOWLY RAISES HIS HAND, WHICH SEEMS TO LEVITATE THE ULTIMATE SWORD!

CLAANG

THE SWORD SHIELD IS CHARGED WITH NAMELESS' IMMENSE CHI. IT IMMEDIATELY KNOCKS THEM BACK!

HE THEN SPINS IT CREATING A SWORD SHIELD TO BLOCK ALL ATTACKS.

WEN WU IS NO SLOUCH AND IS SURPRISED TO BE DEFEATED SO EASILY!

ALL OF A SUDDEN, THE ULTIMATE SWORD CRASHES INTO THE GROUND, ESCAPING NAMELESS' CONTROL.

THE "NAMELESS" FIGHTER HAS SEEN MANY THINGS AND IS STILL SHOCKED...

THIS SWORD IS JUST LIKE CLOUD -- REBELLIOUS TO THE END!

GET THE SWORD!

HAH!

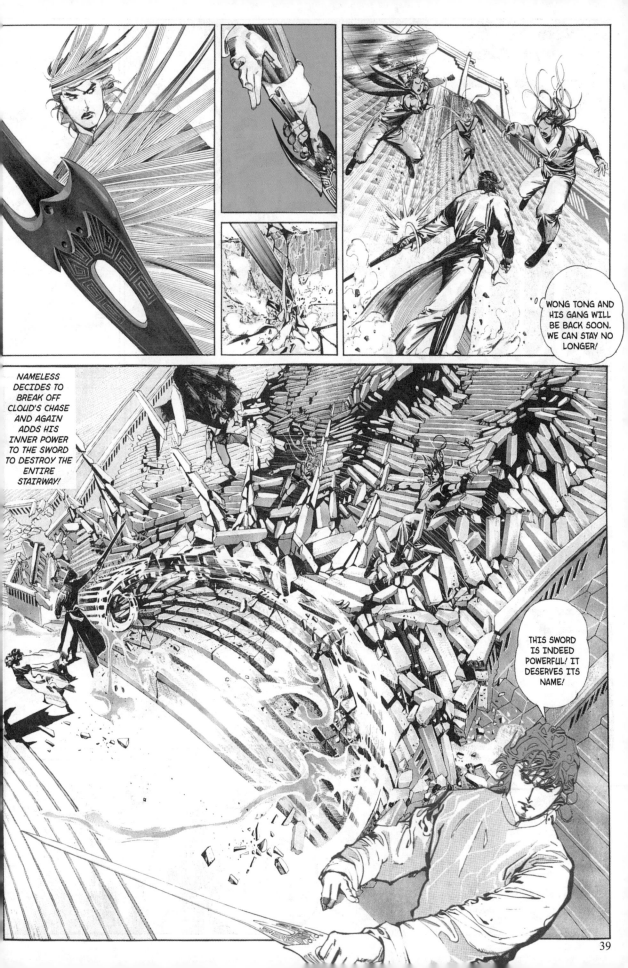

WONG TONG AND HIS GANG WILL BE BACK SOON. WE CAN STAY NO LONGER!

NAMELESS DECIDES TO BREAK OFF CLOUD'S CHASE AND AGAIN ADDS HIS INNER POWER TO THE SWORD TO DESTROY THE ENTIRE STAIRWAY!

THIS SWORD IS INDEED POWERFUL! IT DESERVES ITS NAME!

KOOOM

NAMELESS TAKES YORUO AND FLEES THE SCENE.

THIS POWERFUL EXPLOSION KNOCKS THE THREE BACK!

BAM...
BAM...!

AH! THEY'RE GONE!

NEAR THE CONQUER CLAN -- TIAN YIN CASTLE!

ALRIGHT, I'LL BUY THE HORSE!

THANK YOU!

MISS, LET US GO!

IF I RIDE, WHAT WILL YOU DO?

KLOP
KLOP

HE'S SURE SWIFT ON HIS FEET, EVEN WIND PROBABLY COULDN'T COMPARE!

AH! THERE'S SOMETHING WRONG WITH THE HORSE!

THAT DOESN'T SEEM RIGHT, WE'VE ONLY TRAVELED A FEW MILES, HOW CAN IT GROW TIRED ALREADY?

CRACK

THE HORSE'S FRONT LEGS BREAK AT THEIR JOINTS AS THE ANIMAL CRASHES TO THE GROUND!

CRACK

WHILE YORUO IS FALLING, A BREEZE CATCHES HER!

FWOOO...

THIS BREEZE IS CONTROLLED BY NAMELESS!

WHAT HAPPENED?

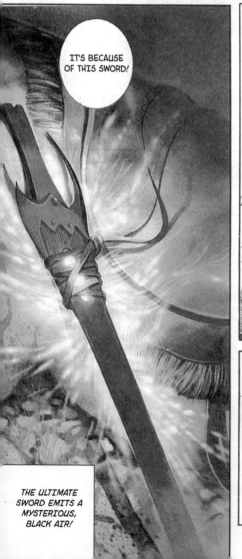

IT'S BECAUSE OF THIS SWORD!

THE ULTIMATE SWORD EMITS A MYSTERIOUS, BLACK AIR!

THIS SWORD WAS MADE FROM VERY SPECIAL METAL. ITS HEART IS CONNECTED TO ITS MASTER CLOUD. IT SUCKS THE ENERGY FROM ITS SURROUNDINGS!

THIS SWORD'S KILLING URGE IS TOO GREAT. I MUST KEEP IT IN A PEACEFUL PLACE FOR IT TO RETURN TO THE RIGHTEOUS PATH!

YOU'RE HOLDING THE SWORD. ISN'T YOUR ENERGY AND POWER BEING ABSORBED BY IT AS WELL?

NAMELESS FEELS IT TOO, THE SWORD IS TRYING TO SUCK HIS ENERGY AND POWER, BUT HE HAS BEEN PROTECTING HIMSELF.

BESIDES, THE ULTIMATE SWORD IS A "NEWBORN," IT CAN'T ABUSE ITS POWERS IN FRONT OF NAMELESS -- AN ANCIENT SWORD!

HE IS CONTROLLING THE SWORD, AS THE BLACK AIR FLOWS BACK INTO IT.

NOW THAT YOU HAVE CLOUD'S SWORD, WHERE'RE YOU GOING?

I'LL BRING YOU TO YOUR FATHER FIRST!

AH! HOW'S MY FATHER DOING? WHERE IS HE?

HE'S DOING FINE. HE'S POWERLESS, BUT HE'S AWAITING YOU TO RESIDE IN PEACE WITH HIM!

YORUO BEGINS TO WEEP AS SHE REMEMBERS HER FATHER CONQUERING THE LANDS. WITH BATTLES EVERYDAY, THERE WAS NEVER ANY PEACE IN HER LIFE.

AS DARKNESS FALLS, THE TWO STAY THE NIGHT AT A LODGE.

THAT'S... WONDERFUL!

LODGE

LIGHTS OUT... DARKNESS FALLS AND SPREADS ACROSS THE ROOM. DARKNESS IS MYSTERIOUS, LIFELESS... AND CAN CONTAIN UNBELIEVABLE POWERS.

DARKNESS, MAKES NAMELESS COLD.

DARKNESS, IS ALSO THE PLACE WHERE CLOUD CAN RECLAIM HIS SWORD!

WHAM

44

WHAT WAS THAT?

BOOM

AH!

CLOUD'S ATTEMPT IS FUTILE!

HE'S... TOO POWERFUL!

CLOUD, GIVE UP! THERE'S NO WAY YOU'LL BE ABLE TO TAKE THIS SWORD!

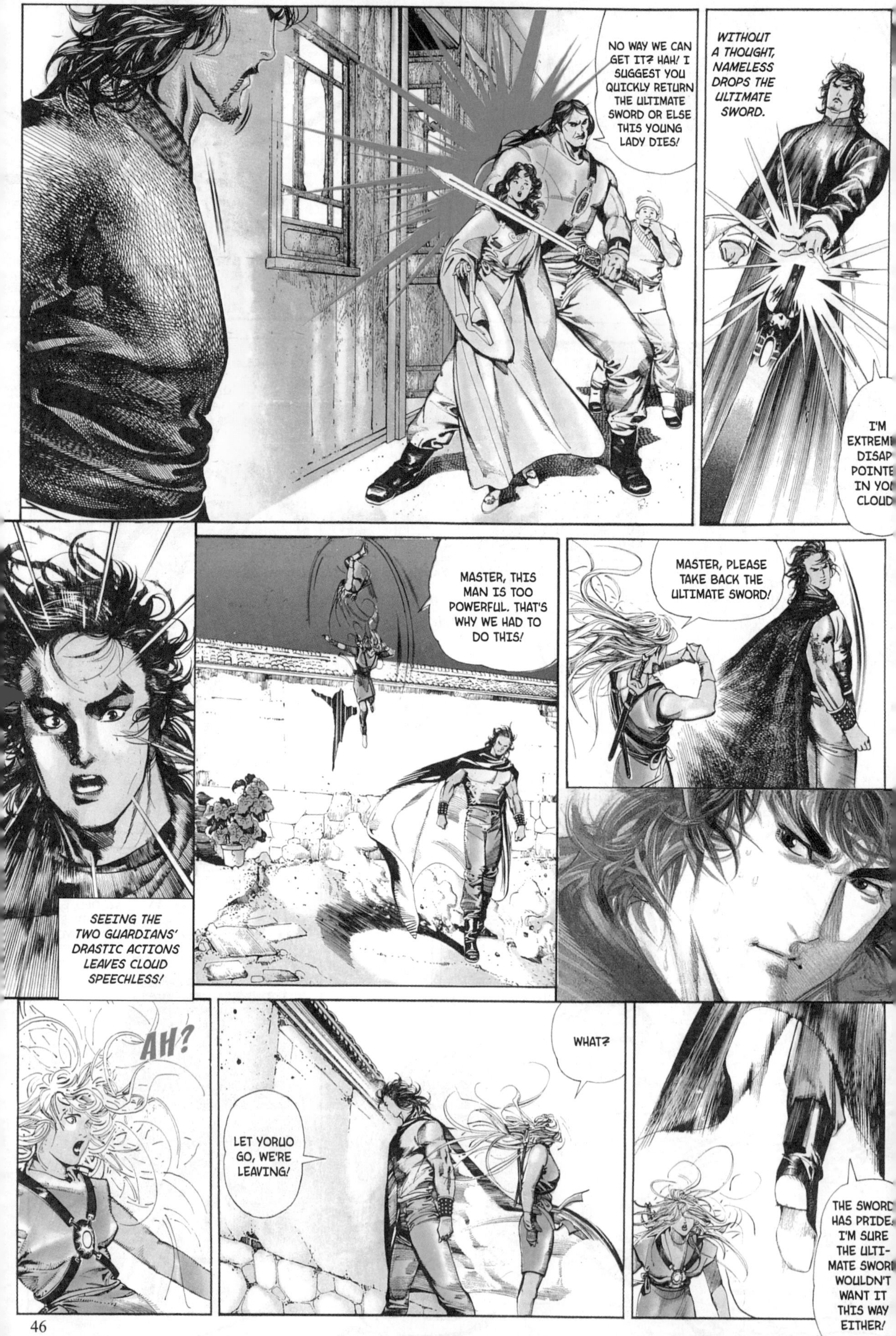
NO WAY WE CAN GET IT? HAH! I SUGGEST YOU QUICKLY RETURN THE ULTIMATE SWORD OR ELSE THIS YOUNG LADY DIES!
WITHOUT A THOUGHT, NAMELESS DROPS THE ULTIMATE SWORD.
SEEING THE TWO GUARDIANS' DRASTIC ACTIONS LEAVES CLOUD SPEECHLESS!
MASTER, THIS MAN IS TOO POWERFUL. THAT'S WHY WE HAD TO DO THIS!
MASTER, PLEASE TAKE BACK THE ULTIMATE SWORD!
AH?
WHAT?
LET YORUO GO, WE'RE LEAVING!

HMM!

TAKING A GIRL HOSTAGE ISN'T SOMETHING A REAL MAN WOULD DO!

CLOUD IS A REAL MAN, WHY WOULD HE JOIN YOU RASCALS IN YOUR LITTLE TRICKS?

WEN WU IS HONORABLE, BUT FELT THE NEED TO DO SOMETHING. HE TOOK YORUO HOSTAGE OUT OF GUILT.

ALRIGHT! WE'LL LET YOU GO THIS TIME. BUT WE'LL GET THE ULTIMATE SWORD BACK!

THE NEXT DAY...

UPON FINDING ANOTHER HORSE FOR YORUO, THEY BEGIN ANEW.

NO MATTER WHERE THEY GO, CLOUD IS ALWAYS NEARBY WATCHING THEIR EVERY MOVE.

SIR, WE'RE MOVING AT SUCH A QUICK PACE. GOING HERE AND THERE... HOW CAN CLOUD STILL KEEP UP WITH US?

HE'S CONNECTED TO THIS SWORD ALREADY, THAT IS WHY HE KNOWS WHERE WE ARE... HE CAN SENSE THE SWORD.

BUT HIS RIVALRY WITH MY FATHER RUNS DEEP. I'M AFRAID IF HE FOLLOWS US AND FINDS WHERE MY FATHER IS, HE WILL BE IN GRAVE DANGER.

............

NAMELESS AND YORUO SELDOM REST AND CHANGE DIRECTIONS REPEATEDLY. NOW THEY HEAD WEST!

THE TWO CONTINUE THEIR JOURNEY AND CLOUD CONTINUES TO FOLLOW. BUT CLOUD IS NOT INTERESTED IN THEIR DESTINATION. HE ONLY WANTS THE SWORD!

IT'S NOT SO EASY TO LOSE ME! I DON'T BELIEVE THAT YOU TWO WON'T GROW TIRED AND NEED TO REST. IN THE END, I WILL HAVE MY SWORD!

NAMELESS ISN'T GETTING MUCH REST EITHER AS HE PROTECTS THE SWORD FROM CLOUD. AFTER SO MANY DAYS OF TRAVELING, THEY END UP AT A BEACH!

HEY, PLEASE WAIT!

IS SOMETHING THE MATTER?

WHY ARE YOU TWO HEADING OVER THERE?

I'M NOT SURE WHY WE'RE GOING THERE.

OH? WHY SO?

THERE'RE TWO MIDDLE-AGED MEN THERE. THEY ARE SO POWERFUL THAT THEY WILL KILL WHOEVER GOES NEAR!

IF THAT'S THE CASE, I SUGGEST NOT GOING NEAR THERE! IT'S DANGEROUS!

DON'T WORRY! NO MATTER HOW POWERFUL THEY ARE, THEY WON'T COME CLOSE TO HARMING HIM!

IT'S BECAUSE OF THESE TWO MEN THAT NAMELESS HAS COME. ONE IS FISHING ON THE EDGE OF THE CLIFF.

ON THE MOUNTAIN IS A HUGE CARVING OF A DRAGON. A CARVING SO LIFELIKE... SO POWERFUL, BUT LACKING COURAGE...!

IT'S BECAUSE THE CARVING ISN'T COMPLETE. THE DRAGON'S EYES AREN'T THERE. WITHOUT ITS EYES, THE DRAGON CANNOT SEE.

THAT DRAGON CARVING IS SO LIFE-LIKE, WHO CARVED IT?

WHO KNOWS? MOTHER SAID THAT TWENTY YEARS AGO THERE WAS A LIGHTNING STORM AND ALL THE FISHERMEN IN THE VILLAGE HEARD A HUGE ROAR -- LIKE A DRAGON!

THE NEXT DAY, THEY FOUND THIS DRAGON ON THE MOUNTAIN SIDE. THEY SAID IT WAS THE DRAGON GOD'S DOING.

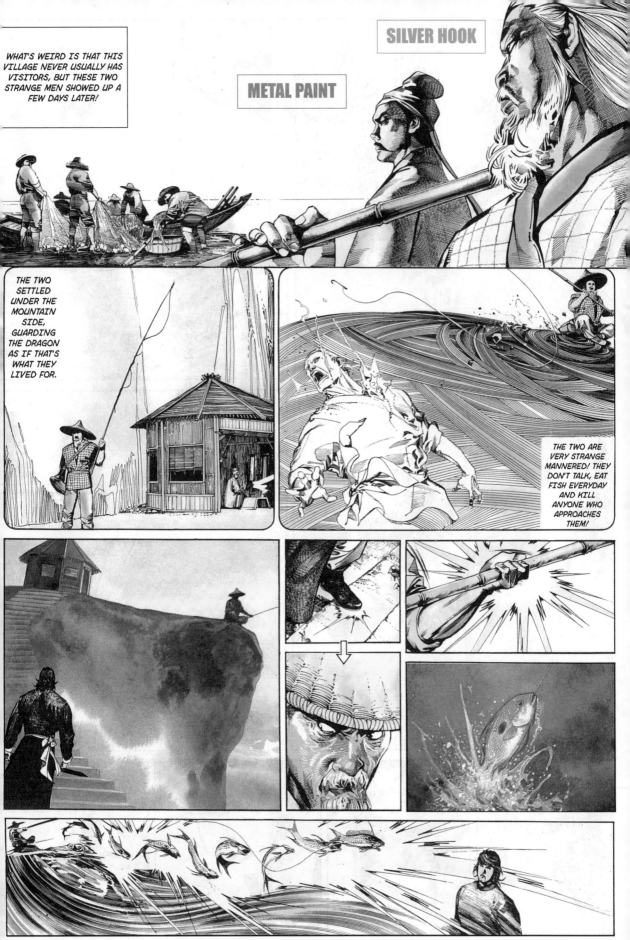

SILVER HOOK

METAL PAINT

WHAT'S WEIRD IS THAT THIS VILLAGE NEVER USUALLY HAS VISITORS, BUT THESE TWO STRANGE MEN SHOWED UP A FEW DAYS LATER!

THE TWO SETTLED UNDER THE MOUNTAIN SIDE, GUARDING THE DRAGON AS IF THAT'S WHAT THEY LIVED FOR.

THE TWO ARE VERY STRANGE MANNERED! THEY DON'T TALK, EAT FISH EVERYDAY AND KILL ANYONE WHO APPROACHES THEM!

51

WITH GREAT FORCE, SILVER HOOK SENDS A FISH FLYING AT NAMELESS LIKE AN ARROW. THE FISH'S MOUTH GLOWS PURPLE, SHOWING IT IS POISONOUS.

NAMELESS TIGHTENS HIS GRIP ON THE SWORD.

AS IF HE DIDN'T MOVE YET, THE FISH SUDDENLY STOPS.

IT HAS ALREADY BEEN CUT TO PIECES!

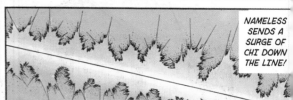

NAMELESS SENDS A SURGE OF CHI DOWN THE LINE!

A FISH LINE IS FLIMSY AND WEAK, BUT WITH NAMELESS' POWERS TRAVELING ON IT, IT IMMEDIATELY BREAKS SILVER HOOK'S WEAPON.

HAH!
HAH!
HAH!

SUCH A POWERFUL OPPONENT!

IT'S METAL PAINT'S TURN. HIS AGE-OLD WEAPON IS A BRUSH!

52

THE BRUSH MAY BE SIMPLE, BUT THE INK ISN'T. FILLED WITH POISON, IT CAN DISINTE-GRATE ALMOST ANYTHING ON CONTACT!

HAH!

WHO ARE YOU? HOW DARE YOU DISRUPT THE DRAGON?

WITH A HOWL, METAL PAINT SWINGS HIS ARM AROUND IN MID-AIR, WRITING THE CHARACTER, "DRAGON!"

DIE!

THE POISON INK HANGS STILL IN MID-AIR, IN THE FORM OF THE CHARACTER FOR DRAGON. IT FLIES TOWARDS NAMELESS, SHOWING THAT METAL PAINT'S SKILLS ARE ABOVE SILVER HOOK'S.

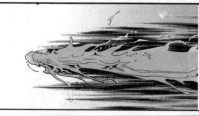

THE CHARACTER SPLITS INTO SEVERAL MINI "INK ARROWS," LIKE LITTLE DRAGONS FLYING AT NAMELESS!

GOOD WORD!

HE SWINGS HIS SWORD AND BLOCKS IT!

THE ULTIMATE SWORD, COMBINED WITH NAMELESS'S POWERS, IS LIMITLESS AND THE POISONOUS INK TURNS INTO A SWIRL!

AH?!

TAP

TAP

AT THE SAME TIME, NAMELESS SENDS TWO STREAMS OF THE TOXIC INK BACK AT METAL PAINT LIKE FLYING SWORDS!

WAH!

54

SHUNK

SHUNK.

METAL PAINT AVOIDS THE KILLING BLOW AS THE TWO STREAMS OF POISONOUS INK LAND AND CREATE THE EYES OF THE DRAGON CARVING. NOW THE DRAGON NOT ONLY LOOKS ALIVE -- BUT FURIOUS!

OH! THE DRAGON'S AWAKE, HE... CAN FINALLY COME BACK!

NAMELESS SLOWLY DRIFTS DOWN FROM MIDAIR LIKE A GOD!

WE'RE SO SORRY! WE DIDN'T KNOW WHO YOU WERE.

METAL PAINT AND SILVER HOOK BOW TO NAMELESS IN JOY AND SHOCK!

THEY'RE SO ODD... THEY JUST LEFT!

I WONDER WHO THEY WERE?

THOSE TWO MEN HAVE GUARDED THE DRAGON FOR OVER TWENTY YEARS... SUCH LOYALTY.

SIR, WHY'D YOU BRING ME HERE? WAS IT JUST TO LET THOSE TWO MEN GO?

MISS YORUO, I THINK WE'LL BE RESTING HERE TONIGHT.

FOR THE LAST TWO DAYS, THEY'VE BEEN AVOIDING CLOUD WITH NO REST. HEARING THIS, YORUO WAS IMMEDIATELY FILLED WITH JOY.

ALRIGHT!

THEN I'LL GO OVER TO THE VILLAGERS TO GET SOME FOOD. THEY SEEM LIKE NICE PEOPLE!

MISS, WHO ARE YOU TWO? WHY DID THOSE TWO STRANGE MEN LEAVE?

I HEAR THAT SOMETHING BIG WILL HAPPEN WHEN THE DRAGON WAKES UP!

YEAH! THOSE TWO STRANGE MEN MAY BRING REINFORCEMENTS. YOU'D BETTER BE CAREFUL!

DON'T WORRY! CAN I ASK SOME OF YOU TO SELL ME SOME FOOD PLEASE?

HEY, YOU HELPED US GET RID OF THOSE STRANGE MEN... WE'LL GIVE YOU FOOD!

NAMELESS STANDS TALL AT THE EDGE OF THE CLIFF, LOOKING OUT INTO THE BIG, DEEP, BLUE SEA.

CRAASH

CLOUD! NO REST FOR THE PAST DAYS... YOUR DEDICATION IS AMAZING. LOOKS LIKE YOU WON'T LET UP!

THE ONLY WAY NOW, IS TO USE WHAT'S IN FRONT OF ME TO LOSE CLOUD FOR SURE!

KLOP ...KLOP ...KLOP ...

AH!

AH! SOME-ONE'S ROB-BING THE COACH!

DON'T WORRY! I'M HERE!

AT THE SAME TIME, TWO MEN SPEEDILY APPROACH THE COACH!

OF THE TWO, ONE IS OLD, AND THE OTHER YOUNG. THE OLD ONE IS IN ROBES, AND THE YOUNG ONE IN BLOOD-RED!

IT'S DUAN-LANG AND SWORD DEMON!

THIS IS NOT GOOD!

DUAN-LANG'S FACE HAS GROWN EVIL, AND THE GLOW IN HIS EYES SHOWS THAT HIS POWERS HAVE INCREASED!

WE WANT THE COACH! GET OUT!

ONLY SILENCE IS HEARD FROM WITHIN THE COACH...

WHO ARE YOU?! I'LL TAKE YOU OUT AND KILL YOU!

WAIT!

I CAN SENSE THAT THERE'S SWORD CHI IN THIS COACH......

THIS SWORD CHI IS ABOVE AVERAGE. USE CAUTION!

OH? THERE'S A POWERFUL SWORDSMAN IN THE COACH? THEN I CAN USE MY NEWLY-LEARNED "BREAKING THE CHI OF SWORD VEINS"!

SUDDENLY, THE TWO BREAK OUT OF THE COACH AND HEAD DOWNHILL!

DUAN-LANG KNEW THEY WOULD FLEE AND FLIES LIKE A FIREBALL IN FRONT OF THE ESCAPEES.

59

THE TWO IN THE COACH WERE ACTUALLY JIEN-CHEN AND CHU CHU, ON THEIR WAY TO FIND CLOUD!

HA, IT'S YOU, THE ONE WHO LOST TO ME, THE NEW "HERO SWORD OWNER," JIEN-CHEN!

DUAN-LANG MAY BE CONFIDENT, BUT HE STILL NEEDS TO READY HIS SWORD.

THESE TWO ARE AS EVIL AS CAN BE, STAY BEHIND ME!

OH, ISN'T THAT GIRL THE ONE WHO FOLLOWS CLOUD AROUND ALL THE TIME? WHY'S SHE WITH YOU? DID SHE DITCH CLOUD?

THAT MAKES SENSE THOUGH! THE NEW OWNER OF THE HERO SWORD IS SO BRAVE AND HANDSOME. IF I HAD A CHOICE I WOULDN'T PICK THAT HEARTLESS CLOUD.

DUAN-LANG! SHUT THE HELL UP!

DON'T BE MAD, JIEN-CHEN!

OH? THIS MAN HAS FEELINGS FOR THE GIRL...

BANG

THROOM

AHH!

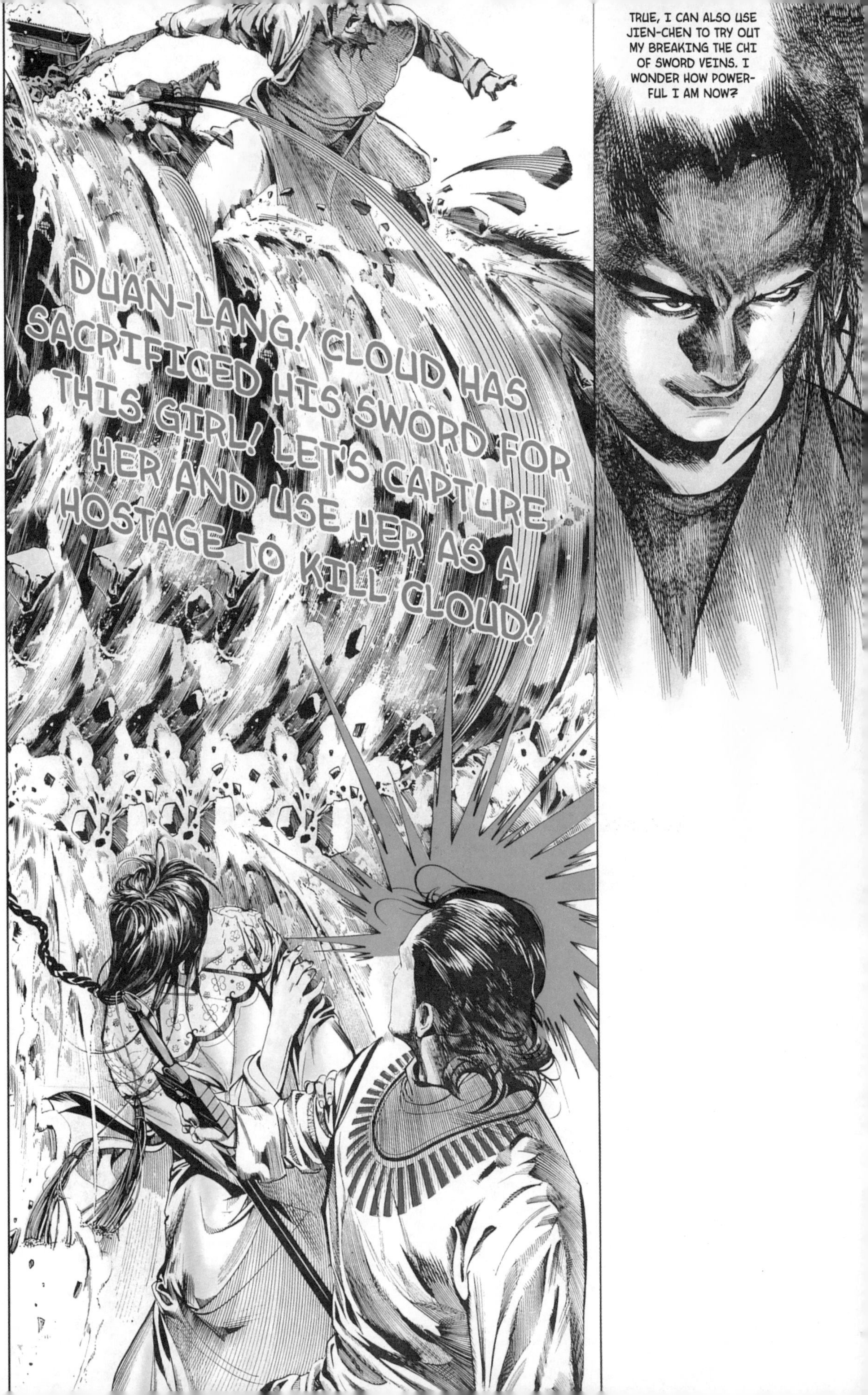
TRUE, I CAN ALSO USE JIEN-CHEN TO TRY OUT MY BREAKING THE CHI OF SWORD VEINS. I WONDER HOW POWERFUL I AM NOW?
DUAN-LANG! CLOUD HAS SACRIFICED HIS SWORD FOR THIS GIRL! LET'S CAPTURE HER AND USE HER AS A HOSTAGE TO KILL CLOUD!

# CHAPTER 58 : HERO'S PRIDE

THE SWORD THAT WILL NEVER BOW DOWN TO ANYTHING... A SWORD SO SHARP, IT CAN CUT THROUGH THE DARKNESS OF THE NIGHT, SPREADING ITS BLACK AURA... BRINGING EVEN MORE DARKNESS THAN BEFORE... THE SWORD THAT FORCED NAMELESS TO TAKE ACTION...

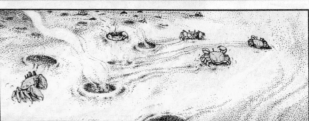

LOOK AT HOW DOMINATING THIS SWORD IS. EVEN THE LITTLE CRITTERS ARE AFRAID OF IT AND HAVE TO MOVE!

THIS SWORD IS TRULY FRIGHTENING. WHAT WILL YOU DO WITH IT?

OH, YOU HAVEN'T SLEPT FOR THE PAST TWO DAYS ALREADY. NO WONDER YOU'VE ALREADY FALLEN ASLEEP.

YOU LIVE TO HELP THE WORLD, TO HELP CLOUD ESCAPE THE EVIL PATH HE'S HEADING TOWARDS. AREN'T YOU TIRED?

FATHER HAS ALWAYS HAD FRIENDS WHO ONLY CARE ABOUT POWER, MONEY AND THEMSELVES. WHEN DID FATHER MEET SOMEONE LIKE YOU?

YORUO SLOWLY AND QUIETLY SNEAKS AWAY FROM NAMELESS AS HE SLEEPS...

HEADING TOWARDS THE DARKEST SHADOWS OF THE NIGHT.

YOU MUST BE STARVED, DO YOU WANT THIS?

CLOUD, I KNOW YOU'RE THERE. I JUST WANT TO ASK HOW WIND IS DOING?

A COLD AND DEEP VOICE TRAVELS OUT OF THE DARKNESS.

HE'S FINE, DON'T WORRY.

I'M GLAD TO HEAR THAT. I HAVEN'T SEEN HIM SINCE HE LEFT THE CONQUER CLAN!

DO YOU KNOW WHERE HE IS? CAN YOU BRING ME TO HIM?

*YORUO WAITS, BUT THERE IS NO REPLY.*

*CLOUD'S PERSONALITY, AND THE FACT THAT HE DOESN'T LIKE TO TALK, WAS KNOWN ACROSS THE CONQUER CLAN. YORUO KNOWS THIS WELL, AND TURNS TO LEAVE.*

YORUO...

WHY ARE YOU WITH HIM? IS HE BRING- ING YOU TO YOUR FATHER?

YORUO NEVER THOUGHT CLOUD WOULD SHOW HIMSELF TO ASK SUCH A QUESTION.

NO! HE... HE'S NOT BRINGING ME TO MY FATHER!

YORUO ANSWERS AND QUICKLY LEAVES.

......

KSSHHHH

WHILE NAMELESS SLEEPS, CLOUDS TAKES THIS OPPORTUNITY TO SEIZE HIS SWORD. BUT THE OCEAN SUDDENLY ROARS AND A HUGE WAVE SLAMS INTO CLOUD, PREVENTING HIM FROM RETRIEVING IT.

ALL OF A SUDDEN, A ROAR COMES FROM THE INCOMING WAVE, A ROAR AS LOUD AS A SLEEPING DRAGON AWAKEN- ING. IN THE MIDDLE OF THIS WAVE COMES NAMELESS' MAIN RIGHT HAND MAN

7 OCEAN DRAGON KING

STRONGER THAN THE FORCE OF A RAGING WAVE, THE DRAGON KING UNLEASHES HIS "DRAGON FORCE FIST" ONTO CLOUD!

EMERGING
FURIOUS
DRAGON

THWAM

THE FORCEFUL WAVE COMES DOWN ONTO NAMELESS, WHO REMAINS CALM AND DRY AS HE EXERTS HIS CHI TO FORM A FORCE FIELD AROUND HIM!

NAMELESS SUDDENLY JUMPS UP!

GRABBING THE SWORD...

CARRYING YORUO...

TOGETHER THEY JUMP OUT OF THE SEA INTO MIDAIR.

69

THE TWO FLOAT OVER TO A SMALL BOAT BY THE SHORESIDE -- AWAY FROM THE FIGHT.

SIR, THAT OLD MAN IS SO POWERFUL, WHO IS HE?

DRAGON FORCE FIST IS SO DOMINATING THAT CLOUD IS UNABLE TO MOUNT AN EFFECTIVE DEFENSE.

I FIGURED SOMETHING WAS WRONG... WHO WOULD'VE THOUGHT IT WAS YOU!

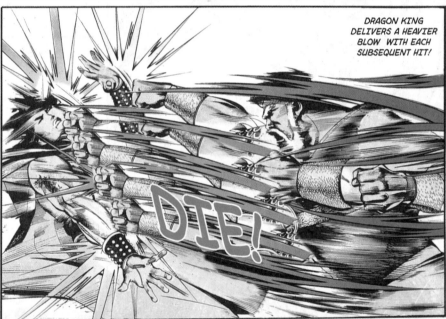

DRAGON KING DELIVERS A HEAVIER BLOW WITH EACH SUBSEQUENT HIT!

DIE!

BUT CLOUD ISN'T WEAK EITHER, HE TAKES A TOTAL OF TEN VIGOROUS HITS BEFORE FALLING BACK.

POW!

POW!

SI!... SI!...

AH! HIS PUNCHES ARE QUITE POWERFUL!

THE PAIN CLOUD IS EXPERIENCING NOW ONLY INCREASES HIS WILL TO FIGHT AS HE TIGHTENS HIS FIST AND IGNITES THE CHI IN HIS BODY.

DRAGON KING DOESN'T CHASE AFTER CLOUD TO CONTINUE THE ATTACK, BUT TRAVELS TO NAMELESS' SIDE.

SORRY I'M LATE, PLEASE FORGIVE ME!

WHEN NAMELESS RETIRED LONG AGO, HE DEPARTED FROM DRAGON KING AT THIS VERY LOCATION. DRAGON KING WAS SO SAD THAT HE CARVED THE DRAGON ON THE MOUNTAIN SIDE, TELLING NAMELESS TO LIGHT THE DRAGONS' EYES IF HE HAD ORDERS FOR HIM.

I HAVE SOMETHING TO TAKE CARE OF AND CANNOT BE DELAYED BY HIM ANYMORE. TAKE CARE OF HIM FOR ME!

DON'T WORRY MASTER! CLOUD IS A SMALL POTATO, I'LL TAKE CARE OF HIM!

OLD MAN, CLOUD USED TO BE A LEADER BACK AT THE CONQUER CLAN, YOU BETTER TAKE CARE!

NAMELESS SENDS A STREAM OF SWORD CHI INTO THE WATER AS THEY BLAST OFF INTO THE OCEAN!

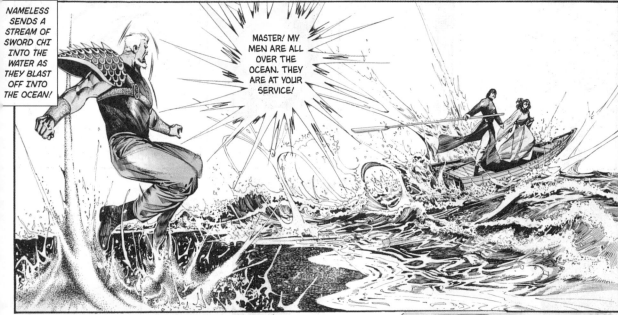

MASTER! MY MEN ARE ALL OVER THE OCEAN. THEY ARE AT YOUR SERVICE!

HOW CAN THIS KID HAVE THE ABILITY TO BOTHER THE MASTER? I BETTER TAKE CAUTION!

ARGH! IGNORANT BOY! YOU MUST GET BY ME IF YOU WANT TO PASS!

SEEING THE BOAT SLOWLY DRIFT FURTHER AND FURTHER, CLOUD FEELS THAT IF HE DOESN'T GET IT BACK NOW, HE'LL NEVER SEE THE ULTIMATE SWORD AGAIN!

AN UNKNOWN POWER GROWS FROM CLOUD AS A BLACK AURA SURROUNDS HIM!

NAMELESS WATCHES FROM AFAR. BUT SEEING CLOUD'S FACE TURN BLACK, HE BEGINS TO WORRY!

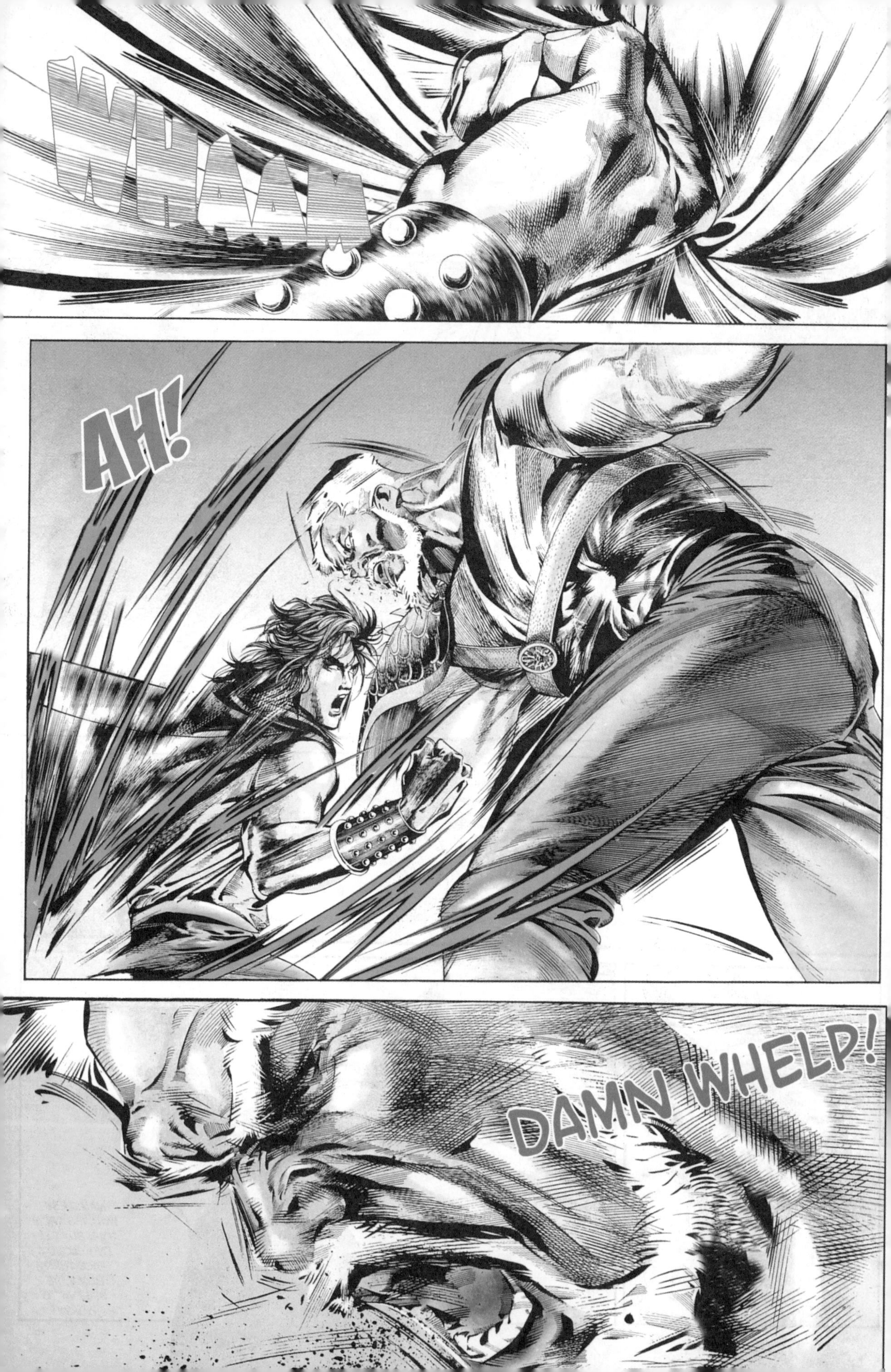
WHAAM
AH!
DAMN WHELP!

**BOOM**

EVEN DRAGON KING WAS KNOCKED BACK INTO THE WAVES FROM CLOUD'S PUNCH!

NAMELESS KNOWS DRAGON KING WELL. HE KNOWS THAT IF HE FIGHTS A STRONGER OPPONENT, HE'LL ONLY GROW STRONGER!

DRAGON KING TURNS HIS HEAD BACK AT CLOUD... A FURIOUS AND DISPLEASED LOOK APPEARS ON HIS FACE!

**AHHH!**

AN ANGRY DRAGON CANNOT BE STOPPED! WITH THE FACT THAT HE'S A KING, HE MUST SHOW HIS OPPO-NENT HIS TRUE POWERS!

BUT THE OPPONENT IS CLOUD, A WARRIOR WHOSE DARED TO CHALLENGE NAMELESS HIMSELF!

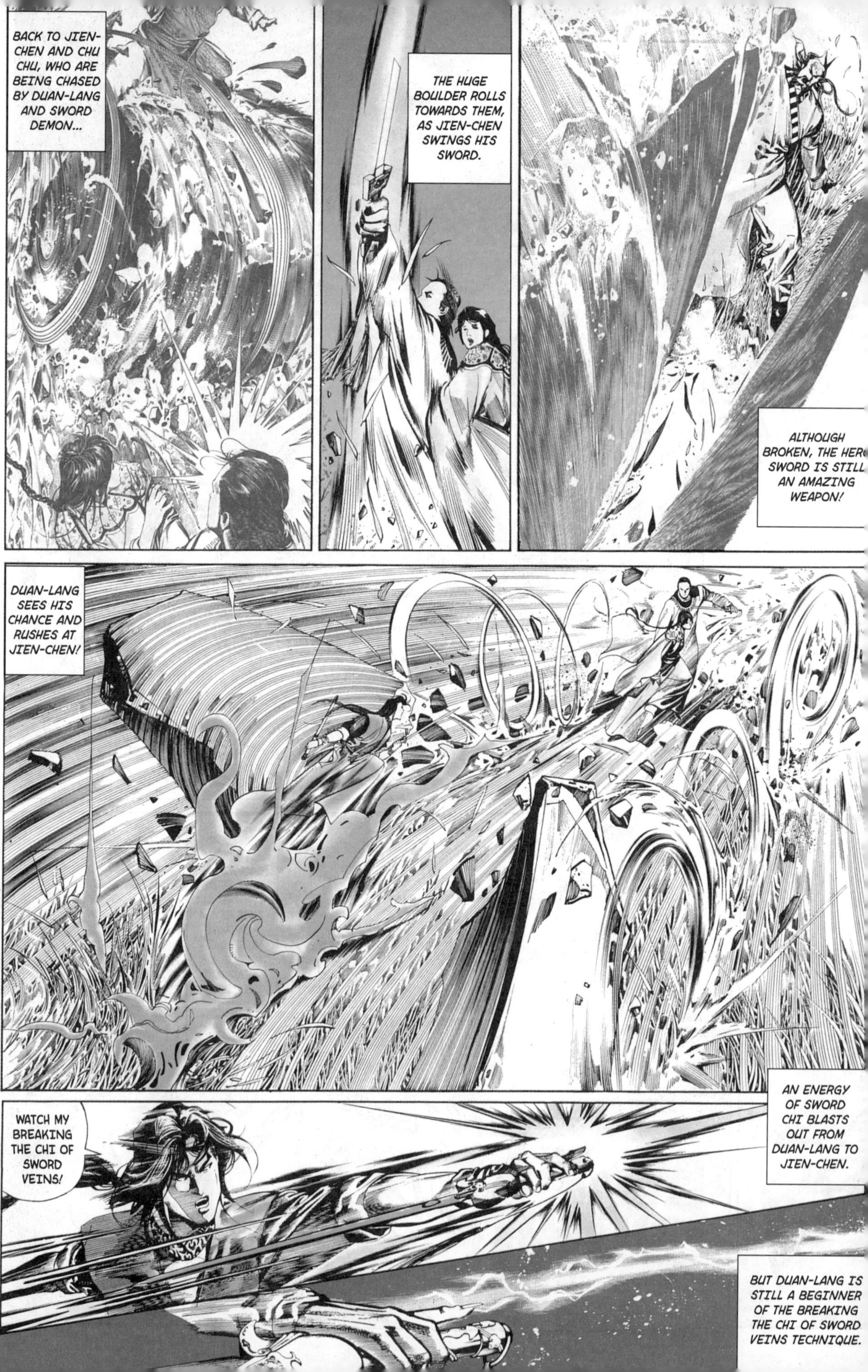
BACK TO JIEN-CHEN AND CHU CHU, WHO ARE BEING CHASED BY DUAN-LANG AND SWORD DEMON...
THE HUGE BOULDER ROLLS TOWARDS THEM, AS JIEN-CHEN SWINGS HIS SWORD.
ALTHOUGH BROKEN, THE HER SWORD IS STILL AN AMAZING WEAPON!
DUAN-LANG SEES HIS CHANCE AND RUSHES AT JIEN-CHEN!
WATCH MY BREAKING THE CHI OF SWORD VEINS!
AN ENERGY OF SWORD CHI BLASTS OUT FROM DUAN-LANG TO JIEN-CHEN.
BUT DUAN-LANG IS STILL A BEGINNER OF THE BREAKING THE CHI OF SWORD VEINS TECHNIQUE.

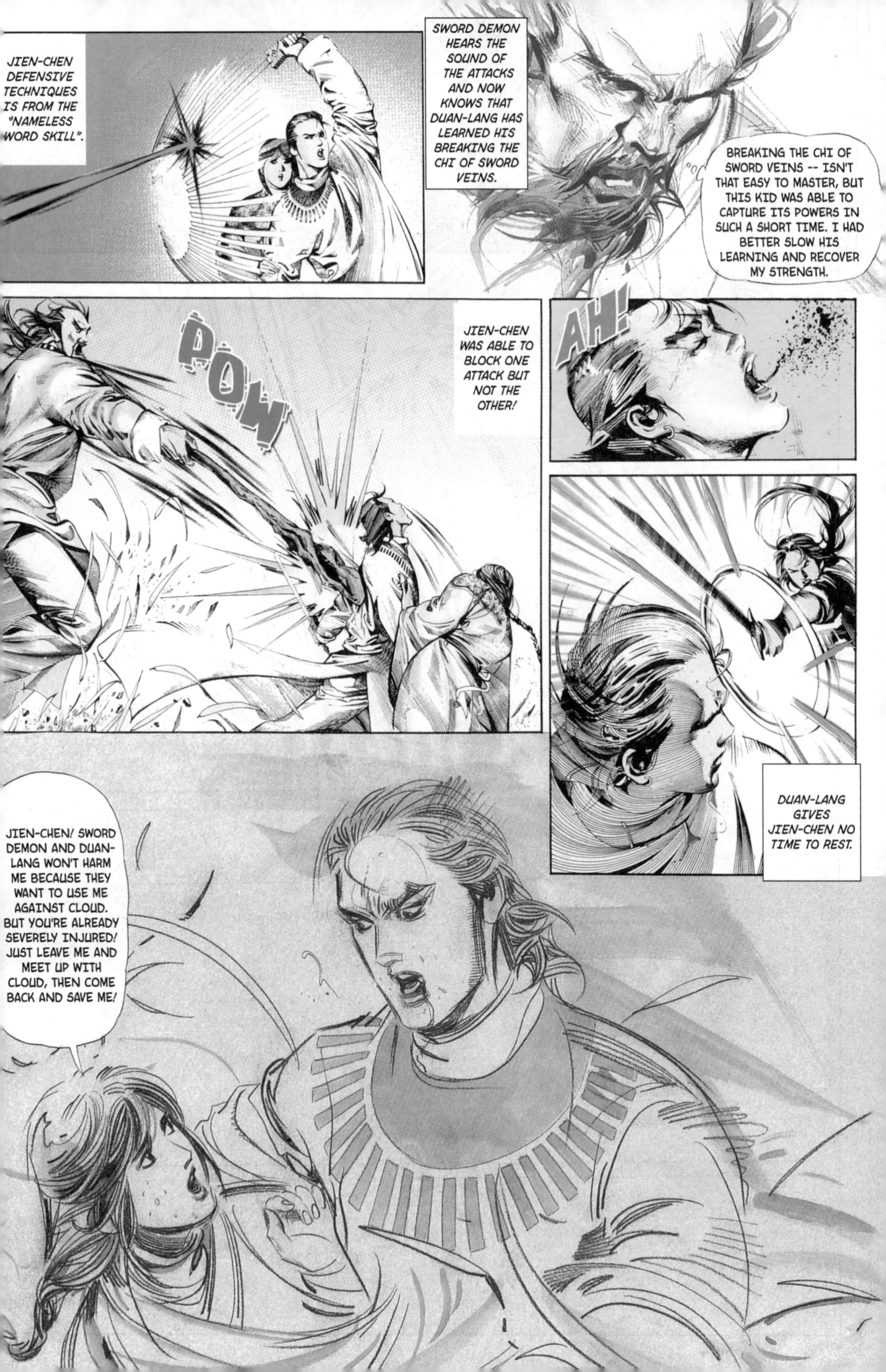
JIEN-CHEN DEFENSIVE TECHNIQUES IS FROM THE "NAMELESS WORD SKILL".
SWORD DEMON HEARS THE SOUND OF THE ATTACKS AND NOW KNOWS THAT DUAN-LANG HAS LEARNED HIS BREAKING THE CHI OF SWORD VEINS.
BREAKING THE CHI OF SWORD VEINS -- ISN'T THAT EASY TO MASTER, BUT THIS KID WAS ABLE TO CAPTURE ITS POWERS IN SUCH A SHORT TIME. I HAD BETTER SLOW HIS LEARNING AND RECOVER MY STRENGTH.
POW
JIEN-CHEN WAS ABLE TO BLOCK ONE ATTACK BUT NOT THE OTHER!
AH!
DUAN-LANG GIVES JIEN-CHEN NO TIME TO REST.
JIEN-CHEN! SWORD DEMON AND DUAN-LANG WON'T HARM ME BECAUSE THEY WANT TO USE ME AGAINST CLOUD. BUT YOU'RE ALREADY SEVERELY INJURED! JUST LEAVE ME AND MEET UP WITH CLOUD, THEN COME BACK AND SAVE ME!

NO! I CAN'T LEAVE YOU BEHIND! WE'LL LEAVE TOGETHER!

THEIR LIVES ARE IN DANGER AND CHU CHU STILL THINKS OF CLOUD. JIEN-CHEN SUDDENLY FEELS A PAIN IN HIS HEART. IS IT JEALOUSY OR ANGER? BOTH ARE FOREIGN TO HIM!

THWACK

WHAM

NAMELESS FIRE SWORD

A NAMELESS FIRE IGNITES WITHIN JIEN-CHEN, IT COMES FROM OUT OF NOWHERE, ALLOWING HIM TO USE THE NAMELESS SWORD SKILL...

INCREDIBLE SWORD CHI RISES UPWARD, SURROUNDING JIEN-CHEN AS EVERY PIECE OF GRASS AROUND BECOMES SHARPER THAN A SWORD. IT IS SO STRONG THAT IT KNOCKS DUAN-LANG AND SWORD DEMON BACK!

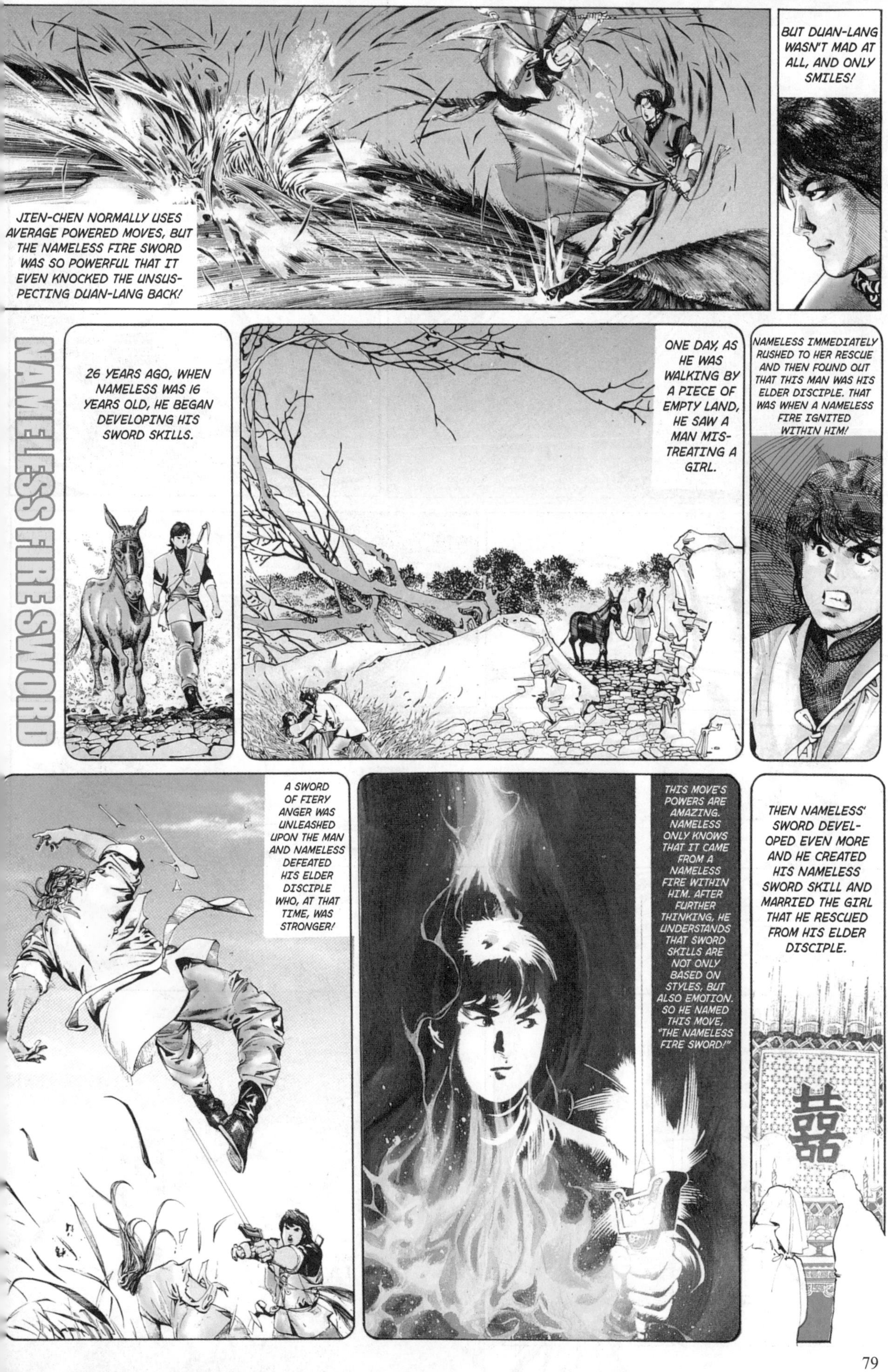
JIEN-CHEN NORMALLY USES AVERAGE POWERED MOVES, BUT THE NAMELESS FIRE SWORD WAS SO POWERFUL THAT IT EVEN KNOCKED THE UNSUSPECTING DUAN-LANG BACK!
BUT DUAN-LANG WASN'T MAD AT ALL, AND ONLY SMILES!
NAMELESS FIRE SWORD
26 YEARS AGO, WHEN NAMELESS WAS 16 YEARS OLD, HE BEGAN DEVELOPING HIS SWORD SKILLS.
ONE DAY, AS HE WAS WALKING BY A PIECE OF EMPTY LAND, HE SAW A MAN MISTREATING A GIRL.
NAMELESS IMMEDIATELY RUSHED TO HER RESCUE AND THEN FOUND OUT THAT THIS MAN WAS HIS ELDER DISCIPLE. THAT WAS WHEN A NAMELESS FIRE IGNITED WITHIN HIM!
A SWORD OF FIERY ANGER WAS UNLEASHED UPON THE MAN AND NAMELESS DEFEATED HIS ELDER DISCIPLE WHO, AT THAT TIME, WAS STRONGER!
THIS MOVE'S POWERS ARE AMAZING. NAMELESS ONLY KNOWS THAT IT CAME FROM A NAMELESS FIRE WITHIN HIM. AFTER FURTHER THINKING, HE UNDERSTANDS THAT SWORD SKILLS ARE NOT ONLY BASED ON STYLES, BUT ALSO EMOTION. SO HE NAMED THIS MOVE, "THE NAMELESS FIRE SWORD!"
THEN NAMELESS' SWORD DEVELOPED EVEN MORE AND HE CREATED HIS NAMELESS SWORD SKILL AND MARRIED THE GIRL THAT HE RESCUED FROM HIS ELDER DISCIPLE.
囍

JIEN-CHEN HAD PLENTY OF ROOM AFTER KNOCKING HIS ENEMIES BACK WITH THE NAMELESS FIRE SWORD, AS HE CARRIES CHU CHU AND ESCAPES FROM DANGER!

AFTER THEM!

THIS JIEN-CHEN HAS VALUE TO ME, I WANT HIM ALIVE!

OH? WHY DID YOU CHANGE YOUR MIND? DO YOU WANT HIS SWORD SKILLS?

CORRECT! I ALREADY HAVE KYLIN AND YOUR BREAKING THE CHI OF SWORD VEINS. IF I WERE TO HAVE HIS NAMELESS SWORD SKILLS TOO, THEN MY SWORD POWER WOULD ONLY INCREASE!

HAH! YOU'RE GREEDIER THAN SWORD NEEDY!

IT'S NOT A MATTER OF GREED, BUT POWER!

WHAT THE?

WHY CAN'T I USE MY CHI?

THERE'S NO WAY THIS KID IS FASTER THAN ME!

DUAN-LANG! STOP WHERE YOU ARE!

HAAH...

SWORD DEMON STOPS AND TRIES TO CIRCULATE HIS CHI.

AH, I'M POISONED!

80

I WON'T DENY IT! I'VE BEEN PUTTING MY FAMILY'S SPECIAL POISON INTO YOUR FOOD. IF YOU DON'T GET MY ANTIDOTE WITHIN A HUNDRED DAYS, YOUR BODY WILL BE EATEN INSIDE-OUT UNTIL YOU DIE A HORRIBLE DEATH!

JUST IN CASE... DON'T WORRY! ONCE YOU AND I TAKE CARE OF CLOUD, THEN I'LL GIVE YOU THE ANTIDOTE!

ENOUGH TALK! WE CANNOT LET JIEN-CHEN ESCAPE!

I UNDERESTIMATED THIS KID!

I'VE ALREADY PASSED MY BREAKING THE CHI OF SWORD VEINS TO YOU... WHY DO THIS TO ME?

AS THE TWO RUN INTO A NEARBY VILLAGE, THEY'VE ALREADY LOST TRACK OF JIEN-CHEN AND CHU CHU. ALL THEY SEE ARE TWO ROADS IN FRONT OF THEM --ONE BIG AND ONE SMALL!

JIEN-CHEN IS THE HERO SWORD'S NEW OWNER, HE WOULDN'T RUIN HIS REPUTATION AND TAKE THE SMALL ROAD...

NORMALLY YOUR ASSESSMENT OF JIEN-CHEN WOULD BE CORRECT. BUT YOU FORGOT TO CONSIDER SOMETHING YOU DON'T HAVE — EMOTION!

EMOTION?

RIGHT, I USE TO NOT CARE ABOUT EMOTIONS EITHER, BUT IN THE END, THEY CAUSED MY DOWNFALL! JIEN-CHEN IS RISKING HIS LIFE FOR THAT YOUNG GIRL, SHOWING THAT HE HAS FEELINGS FOR HER. HE'LL SACRIFICE EVERYTHING, INCLUDING HIS REPUTATION!

SO, JIEN-CHEN DOESN'T CARE ABOUT HIS REPUTA-TION AND TOOK THE SMALL ROAD TO SAVE HER?

THAT'S RIGHT!

OKAY! I'LL TRUST YOU THIS ONE TIME, WE'LL TAKE THE SMALL ROAD!

BUT EVEN SWORD DEMON HAS UNDERESTI-MATED JIEN-CHEN'S FEELINGS TOWARDS CHU CHU.

NEARBY, IN A STINKY, FILTHY PIG STALL, TWO SHADOWS HIDE AWAY.

THESE TWO PEOPLE ARE ACTUALLY JIEN-CHEN AND CHU CHU! JIEN-CHEN INJURIES WERE EXASPERATED WHEN HE FORCED HIS NAMELESS FIRE SWORD.

CHU CHU OVERHEARD SWORD DEMON AND SHE BLUSHES LIGHTLY AS SHE LOOKS AT JIEN-CHEN.

JIEN-CHEN LIGHTLY NODS HIS HEAD.

SHE IS SPEECHLESS WITH EMBARRASSMENT.

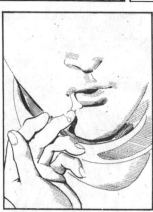

OH?

SWORD CHI?

?

83

BACK TO THE BEACH... CLOUD DELIVERED A HEAVY BLOW TO DRAGON KING AND IN RETURN, DRAGON KING UNLEASHES HIS DRAGON FORCE FIST'S MOST POWERFUL MOVE --

# THUNDEROUS RAGING DRAGON

THE NUMEROUS FISTS COME TOO FAST AS THEY LAND. ALL HE SEES ARE NUMEROUS THUNDER STRIKES RAINING DOWN ON HIM!

HOWEVER, CLOUD'S SACRIFICE IS GREAT IN EXCHANGE FOR THOSE TWO BLOWS!

BUT CLOUD ISN'T WEAK EITHER AS HE RETURNS A HEAVY HIT ONTO DRAGON KING'S SHOULDERS!

BOOM

CLOUD'S POWERFUL STRIKES FORCE DRAGON KING TO REST AND RECOVER.

SHHH...

AH!

CLOUD DIDN'T EVEN BOTHER TO RECOVER AS HIS PALM ATTACK IS INCOMING!

ONCE AGAIN, CLOUD IGNORES THE PAIN AND RETURNS ANOTHER BLOW -- THIS TIME, A KICK TO DRAGON KING'S CHEST!

EACH LANDS A HEAVY BLOW!

AS DRAGON KING FEELS THE PAIN ON HIS CHEST, HE RUNS HIS CHI THROUGHOUT HIS BODY AND USES HIS SPECIAL TECHNIQUE --

ROAR

DRAGON ROAR!

DRAGON ROAR IS AN INTERNAL SKILL THAT TRANSFORMS SOUND INTO A FORM OF ACTIVE CHI THAT TRAVELS THROUGH THE ENEMY, CAUSING GREAT INTERNAL DAMAGE.

CLOUD FEELS UNENDING PAIN AS BLOOD BURSTS OUT FROM HIS MOUTH!

THE PAIN IS SO GREAT IT NEARLY CAUSES CLOUD TO BLACK OUT...

AS HE USES THE TREES TO PULL HIMSELF BACK UP.

87

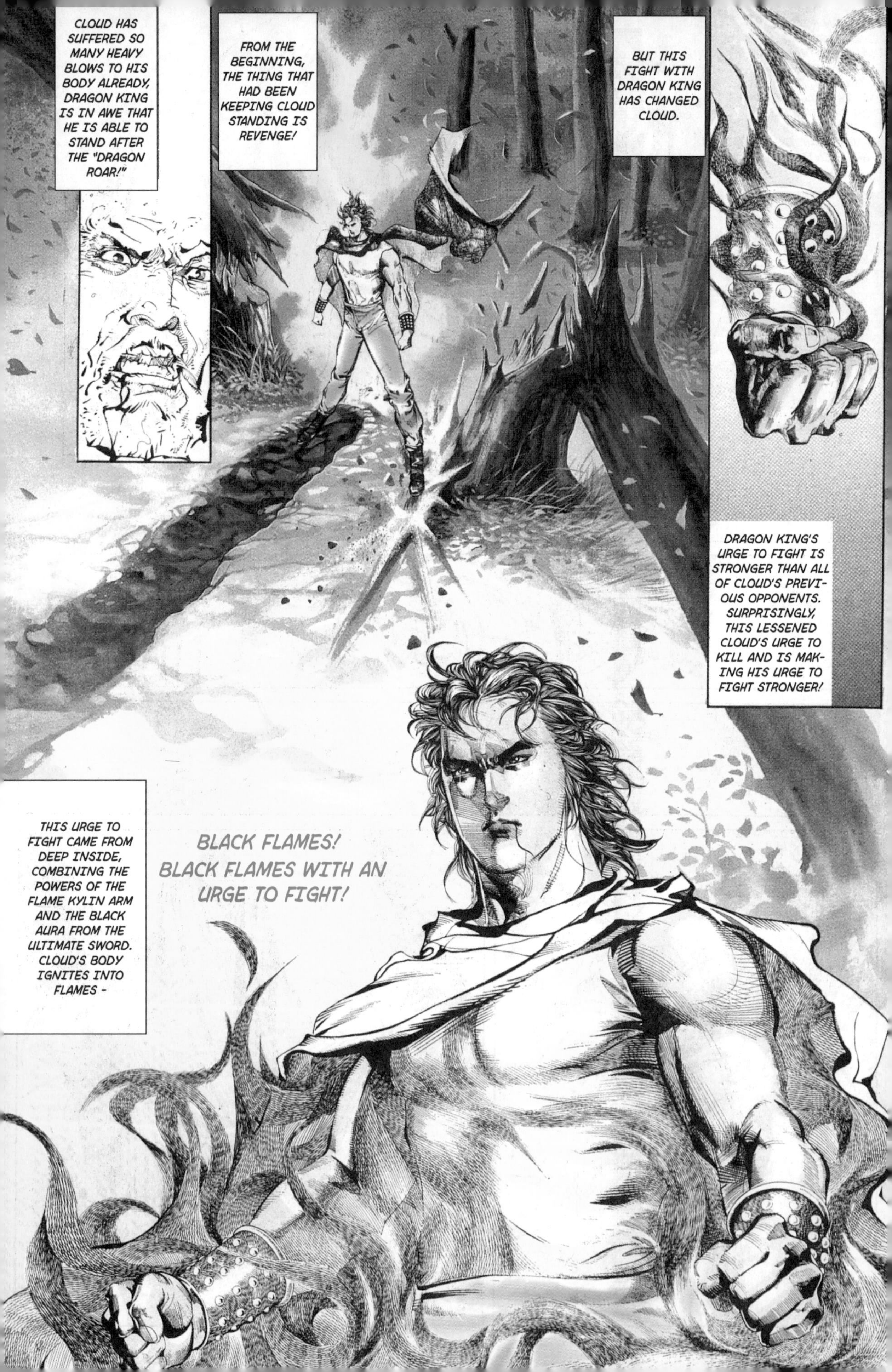
CLOUD HAS SUFFERED SO MANY HEAVY BLOWS TO HIS BODY ALREADY, DRAGON KING IS IN AWE THAT HE IS ABLE TO STAND AFTER THE "DRAGON ROAR!"
FROM THE BEGINNING, THE THING THAT HAD BEEN KEEPING CLOUD STANDING IS REVENGE!
BUT THIS FIGHT WITH DRAGON KING HAS CHANGED CLOUD.
DRAGON KING'S URGE TO FIGHT IS STRONGER THAN ALL OF CLOUD'S PREVI-OUS OPPONENTS. SURPRISINGLY, THIS LESSENED CLOUD'S URGE TO KILL AND IS MAK-ING HIS URGE TO FIGHT STRONGER!
THIS URGE TO FIGHT CAME FROM DEEP INSIDE, COMBINING THE POWERS OF THE FLAME KYLIN ARM AND THE BLACK AURA FROM THE ULTIMATE SWORD. CLOUD'S BODY IGNITES INTO FLAMES -
BLACK FLAMES! BLACK FLAMES WITH AN URGE TO FIGHT!

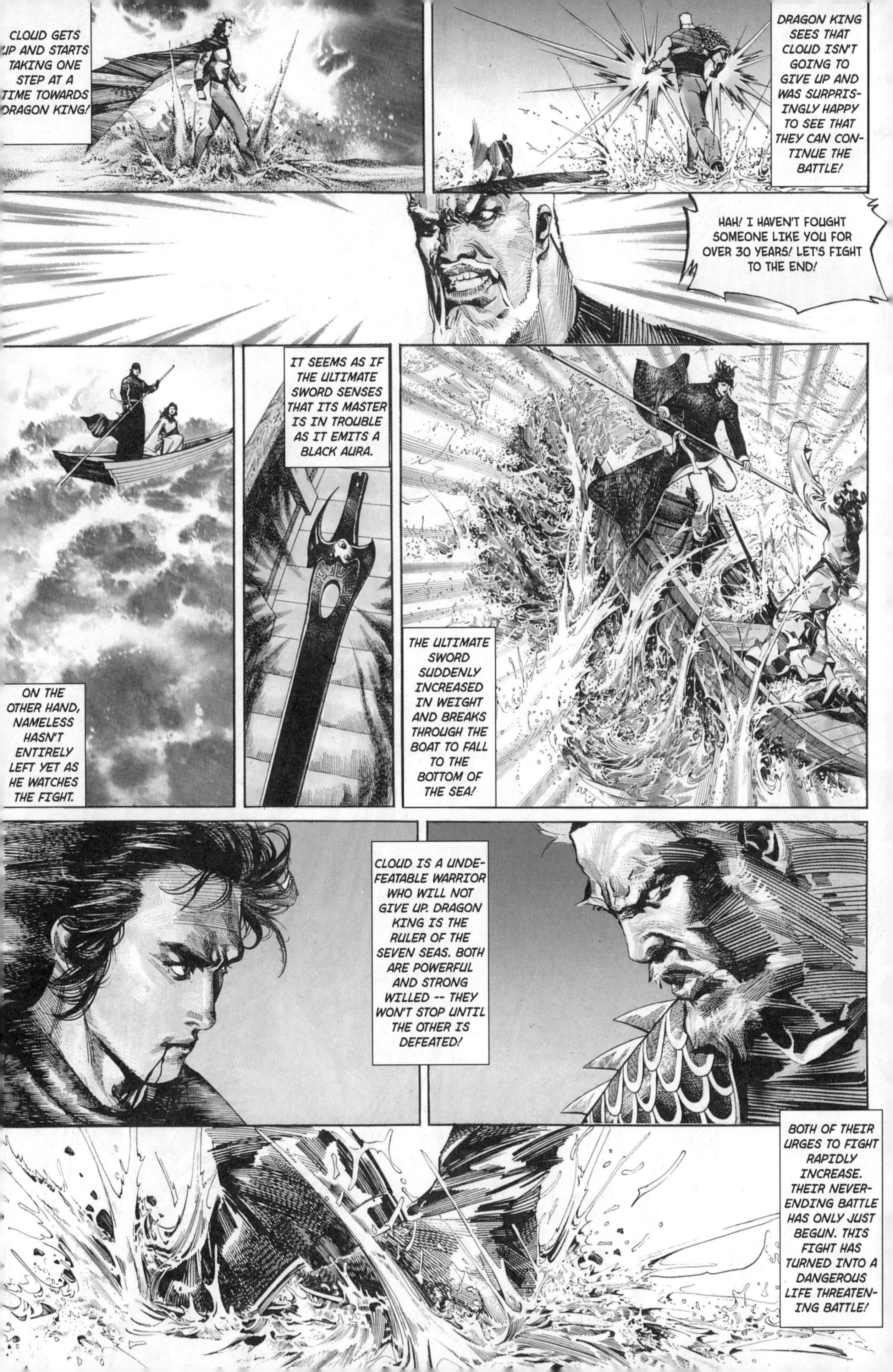
CLOUD GETS UP AND STARTS TAKING ONE STEP AT A TIME TOWARDS DRAGON KING!
DRAGON KING SEES THAT CLOUD ISN'T GOING TO GIVE UP AND WAS SURPRISINGLY HAPPY TO SEE THAT THEY CAN CONTINUE THE BATTLE!
HAH! I HAVEN'T FOUGHT SOMEONE LIKE YOU FOR OVER 30 YEARS! LET'S FIGHT TO THE END!
ON THE OTHER HAND, NAMELESS HASN'T ENTIRELY LEFT YET AS HE WATCHES THE FIGHT.
IT SEEMS AS IF THE ULTIMATE SWORD SENSES THAT ITS MASTER IS IN TROUBLE AS IT EMITS A BLACK AURA.
THE ULTIMATE SWORD SUDDENLY INCREASED IN WEIGHT AND BREAKS THROUGH THE BOAT TO FALL TO THE BOTTOM OF THE SEA!
CLOUD IS A UNDEFEATABLE WARRIOR WHO WILL NOT GIVE UP. DRAGON KING IS THE RULER OF THE SEVEN SEAS. BOTH ARE POWERFUL AND STRONG WILLED -- THEY WON'T STOP UNTIL THE OTHER IS DEFEATED!
BOTH OF THEIR URGES TO FIGHT RAPIDLY INCREASE. THEIR NEVERENDING BATTLE HAS ONLY JUST BEGUN. THIS FIGHT HAS TURNED INTO A DANGEROUS LIFE THREATENING BATTLE!

CLOUD COMBINES HIS POWERS ALONG WITH THE BLACK AURA AROUND HIM TO DELIVER THIS FULL POWERED PUNCH. DRAGON KING USES ALL HIS MIGHT AS WELL TO BRING FORTH THE STRONGEST PUNCH OF HIS DRAGON FORCE FIST. THESE SINGLE ATTACKS WILL DETERMINE THE OUTCOME OF THIS FIGHT!

# CHAPTER 59 : LIFE FOR SWORD

DRAGON KING WAS
ORDERED TO STOP
CLOUD FROM
FOLLOWING
NAMELESS, BUT THE
TWO HAVE STARTED A
BATTLE THAT CANNOT
BE STOPPED NOW.
EACH DELIVERS
THEIR MOST
POWERFUL BLOW.

K.SH... K.SH...

K.SH... K.SH...

**BANG**

ON CONTACT, THE SAND AND OCEAN WATER BLAST INTO THE SKY AS THE TWO FLY BACKWARDS. THEIR POWERS ARE EVENLY MATCHED!

DRAGON KING FEELS AS IF HIS BODY IS BEING BURNED TO A CRISP BY THE BLACK FLAME!

AS HE LANDS INTO THE SEA, THE OCEAN PARTS FOR A FEW MOMENTS!

THE OCEAN WATER IMMEDIATELY EVAPORATES, SHOWING THE SHEER MIGHT OF CLOUD'S ATTACK!

CLOUD'S SUFFERING IS NO LESS AS HE IS SENT REELING!

AS CLOUD LANDS IN THE SANDS, HE IS BURIED BY IT FORMING A SMALL HILL.

`KSH`... `KSH`...

AT THE SAME TIME, DRAGON KING IS BENEATH THE OCEAN, AS A STREAK OF BLOOD APPEARS ON THE SURFACE ALONG WITH THE ULTIMATE SWORD'S RISING BLACK AURA!

THEN, THE PEACEFUL SURFACE IS DISTURBED AGAIN...

DRAGON KING STILL LIVES. HE RISES FROM THE SEA, BUT HIS MOVEMENTS ARE EXTREMELY SLOW, SHOWING THE EXTENT OF HIS INJURIES.

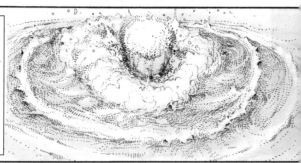

HE WAS COVERED WITH THE BLACK AURA, WHICH TURNS HIS BODY BLACK AS IF HE HAS BEEN BURNED OVER AND OVER AGAIN.

YOU'RE POWERFUL CLOUD! I CAN'T BELIEVE MASTER GAVE ME A TASK THIS TOUGH FOR MY RETURN. WHAT A TEST!! HA HA...

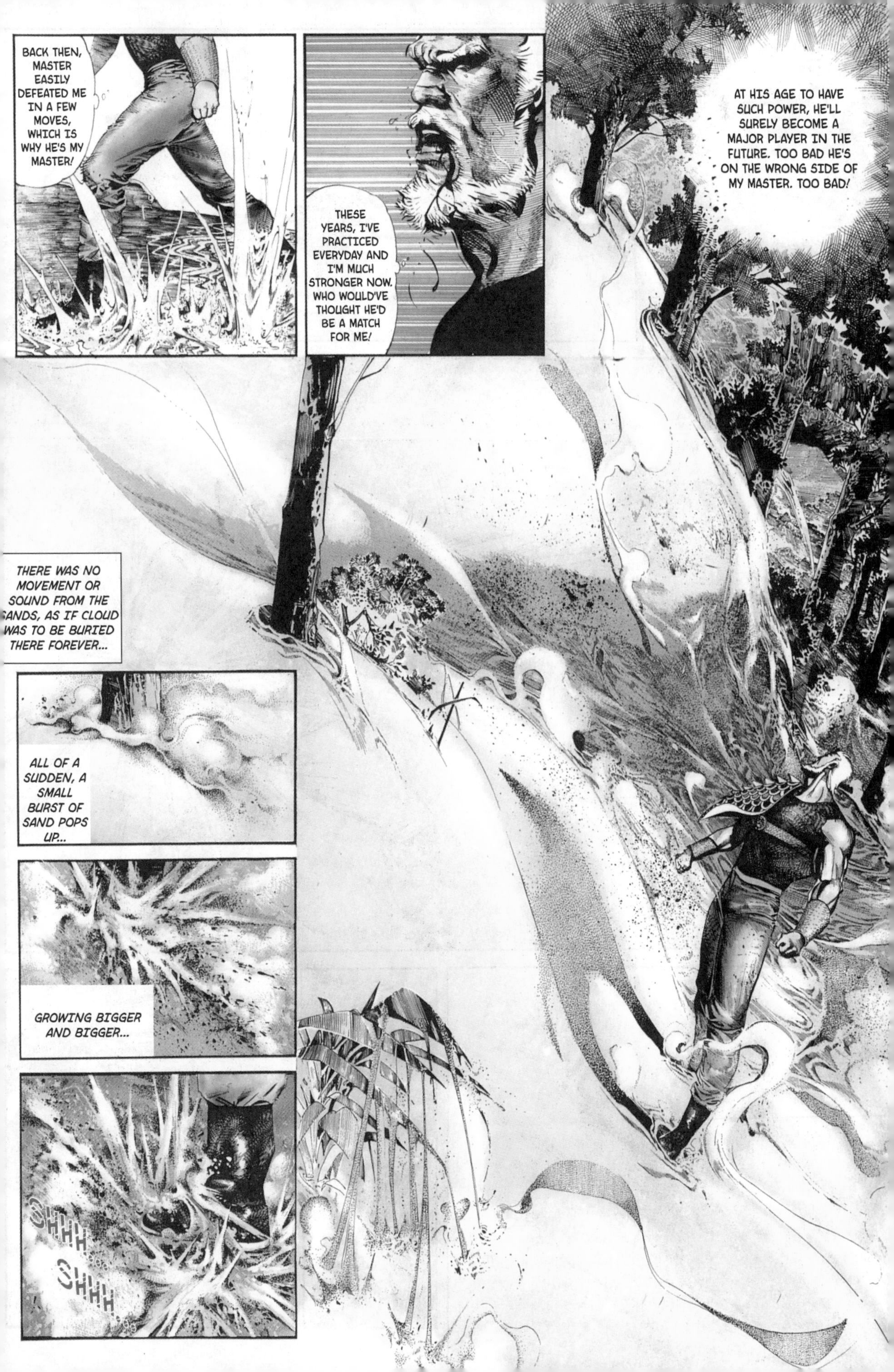
BACK THEN, MASTER EASILY DEFEATED ME IN A FEW MOVES, WHICH IS WHY HE'S MY MASTER!
THESE YEARS, I'VE PRACTICED EVERYDAY AND I'M MUCH STRONGER NOW. WHO WOULD'VE THOUGHT HE'D BE A MATCH FOR ME!
AT HIS AGE TO HAVE SUCH POWER, HE'LL SURELY BECOME A MAJOR PLAYER IN THE FUTURE. TOO BAD HE'S ON THE WRONG SIDE OF MY MASTER. TOO BAD!
THERE WAS NO MOVEMENT OR SOUND FROM THE SANDS, AS IF CLOUD WAS TO BE BURIED THERE FOREVER...
ALL OF A SUDDEN, A SMALL BURST OF SAND POPS UP...
GROWING BIGGER AND BIGGER...
SHHH
SHHH

AH!

THE SANDS RAISE UP...!

DRAGON KING SEES A MOVEMENT IN THE SANDS AND IS FILLED WITH JOY!

HE FEELS THE UNDYING URGE TO FIGHT FROM THE SANDS!

COME ON OUT CLOUD, LET US FIGHT ONCE AGAIN!

OKAY!

DRAGON ANSWERS WITH A FULL-POWERED DRAGON FORCE FIST!

JUST BEFORE THEY CONNECT, A SHADOW APPEARS IN BETWEEN THEM!

THE SHADOW IS NAMELESS!

DRAGON KING IMMEDIATELY DRAWS BACK!

CLOUD WAS SHOCKED TO SEE NAMELESS IN FRONT OF HIM!

HIS TRAINING IS NOT AS ADVANCED AS DRAGON KING'S AND HE IS NOT ABLE TO WITHDRAW HIS ATTACK!

NAMELESS MAKES HIS MOVE.

BOOM

WITH A SIMPLE TAP ON CLOUD'S FIST, NAMELESS SENDS IT EXPLODING INTO THE SANDS!

NAME-LESS KNOWS THAT CLOUD WANTED TO STOP BUT COULDN'T.

CLOUD RETREATS SEVERAL STEPS AS HE TRIES TO CALM DOWN FROM THE SHOCK!

BLOOD BURSTS OL FROM CLOUD'S MOUTH, HI INJURIES ARE FAR MORE SEVERE THAN HE THOUGHT THEY WERE

DRAGON KING, THE ULTIMATE SWORD FELL INTO THE SEA, GET IT BACK FOR ME... PLEASE!

YES MASTER!

FWOOO...

NAMELESS DIDN'T WANT TO SEE EITHER ONE DIE, SO HE HAD TO STOP THE FIGHT.

CLOUD, WILL YOU REALLY DO WHATEVER IT TAKES TO GET THE SWORD BACK?

CLOUD LIGHTLY NODS HIS HEAD AS HE WONDERS WHAT NAMELESS IS UP TO.

ALRIGHT, I'LL GIVE YOU A CHANCE TO GET IT BACK!

MEANWHILE, SWORD DEMON SENSES SWORD CHI COMING FROM THE PIG STALL...

HE'S CERTAIN THAT JIEN-CHEN AND CHU CHU ARE IN THERE!

SWORD DEMON, WHAT'S THE MATTER?

DUAN-LANG POISONED ME. IF HE WERE TO GET THE NAMELESS SWORD SKILL AS WELL, IT'LL BE HARDER FOR ME TO GET BACK AT HIM IN THE FUTURE. THERE'S NO GOOD IN IT FOR ME!

NOTHING, LET'S GO!

SWORD DEMON DECIDED NOT TO HELP DUAN-LANG AND LET JIEN-CHEN GO!

DUAN-LANG FEELS THAT THIS IS ODD, BUT FOLLOWS SWORD DEMON ANYWAYS.

SWORD DEMON AND DUAN-LANG LEAVE. BUT JIEN-CHEN AND CHU CHU REMAIN, AS JIEN-CHEN CIRCULATES HIS CHI TO SPEED UP HIS RECOVERY.

OINK!

AS JIEN-CHEN RESTS, THE PIGS IN THE STALL ARE EXTREMELY UNSTABLE!

JIEN-CHEN FINDS IT STRANGE, BUT CHU CHU IS HAPPY ABOUT IT.

I'VE SEEN OTHER ANIMALS ACT THE SAME WAY WHEN CLOUD IS AROUND...

THAT MEANS CLOUD MUST BE NEAR!

CHU CHU STEPS OUT OF THE PIG STALL BUT DIDN'T SEE CLOUD.

CAREFUL, IT MAYBE DUAN-LANG'S TRICK!

NO WAY! CLOUD CAN'T BE IMPERSONATED LIKE THAT!

ALRIGHT, THEN I'LL GO FIND HIM WITH YOU!

COO.... COO....

LOOK! CLOUD'S PROBABLY OVER THERE!

THE TWO RUN DOWN THE BIG ROAD LOOKING FOR CLOUD.

A SMALL TEA SHOP IS ON THIS BIG ROAD.

HERE, SITS NAMELESS, YORUO, AND NOT FAR, IS CLOUD.

CLOUD REALLY IS HERE!

AH, MASTER?

CLOUD, AM I GLAD TO SEE YOU, I WAS WORRIED!

GREETINGS, MASTER!

JIEN-CHEN, WHY ARE YOU HERE?

JIEN-CHEN TELLS NAMELESS ABOUT CHU CHU'S REQUEST.

BUT HE IS UNEASY AS HE SPEAKS.

CLOUD, YOU'RE HURT AGAIN. WHO DID THIS TO YOU?

SIGH! WHY DOES IT SEEM LIKE YOUR LIFE IS JUST NONSTOP FIGHTING... NEVER ENDING PAIN? WHY CAN'T YOU SETTLE DOWN AND REST?

LET ME CLEAN YOU UP!

CLOUD... THAT HURTS! LET ME GO!

CLOUD, WHAT'RE YOU DOING? LET GO OF MISS CHU CHU!

PAK!

CHU CHU WAS ONLY CONCERNED FOR CLOUD, BUT IN RETURN SHE IS HEARTLESSLY PUSHED ASIDE!

AHH!

MISS CHU CHU!

OH!

THAT'S TOO MUCH! MISS CHU CHU WENT THROUGH HELL TO FIND YOU... TO MAKE SURE YOU'RE SAFE. SHE WAS IN DANGER, ALL FOR YOU!

TO THINK EVERYTHING WOULD BE OKAY WHEN WE FOUND YOU, BUT YOU END UP TREATING HER LIKE THIS... ARE YOU NOT HUMAN?

NAMELESS CAN SEE THAT HIS STUDENT HAS MATURED AND THIS IS SOMETHING HE CANNOT INTERFERE WITH.

JIEN-CHEN....

OH, MASTER!

BANG!

WHERE'RE YOU BRINGING ME? TELL ME!

CLOUD, YOU'VE FOLLOWED ME TO SO MANY PLACES ALREADY, WHY ARE YOU STILL SO IMPATIENT? IF YOU MUST KNOW, WE'RE GOING TO THE "FORESTALL TEMPLE"!"

AS THEY ENTERED THE "SAD BUDDHA HALL", THEY ALL CAN SEE FORESTALL TEMPLE IS A SACRED PLACE.

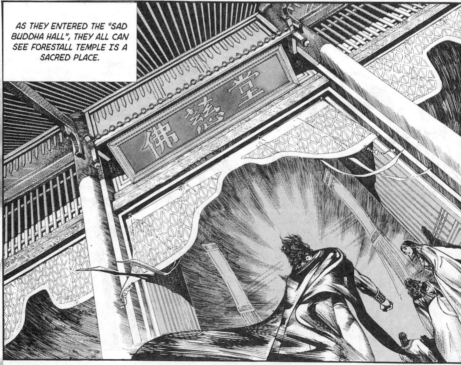

ABOVE EVERYTHING ELSE IS A HUGE STATUE OF A BUDDHA, WITH A FACE BOTH HAPPY AND SAD ITS EXPRESSION IS SO PEACEFUL THAT IT BRINGS CALM TO EVERYONE AROUND IT.

IN THE MIDDLE OF THE PEACEFUL HALL, IS SOMEONE WHO IS THE EXACT OPPOSITE -- SOMEONE WHO HOLDS A BLACK AURA FILLED WITH AN URGE TO KILL; THIS PERSON IS CLOUD!

HE'S FOLLOWED NAMELESS FOR SO LONG NOW AND HAS FINALLY ARRIVED.

WHY DID YOU BRING ME HERE?

IT'S SIMPLE, I WILL MAKE A DEAL WITH YOU; IF YOU BEAT ME, YOU CAN HAVE THE SWORD BACK!

FOOM

NAMELESS SLOWLY RAISES HIS ARM AND SENDS THE ULTIMATE SWORD FLYING!

SHING

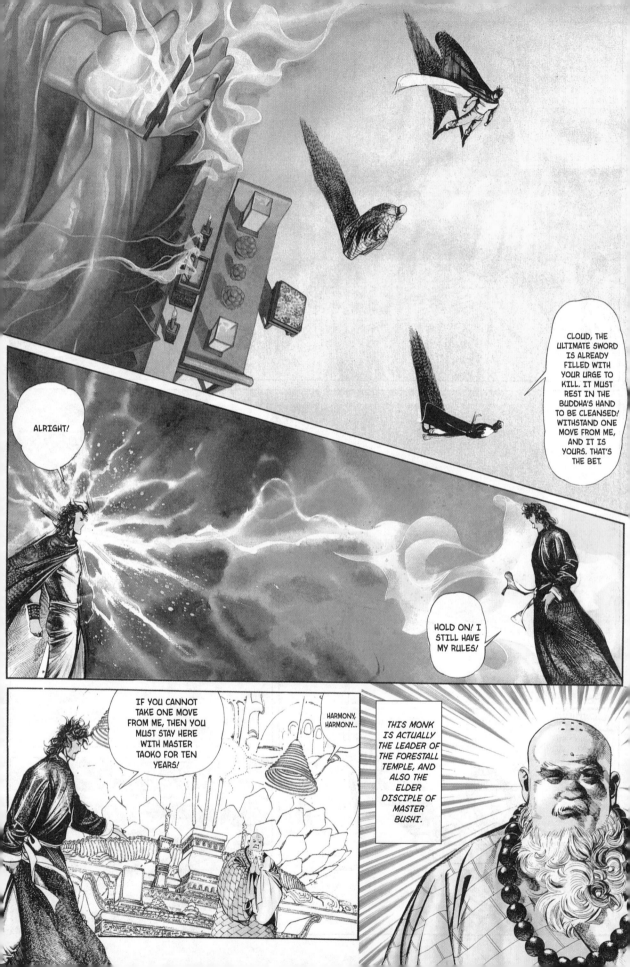

CLOUD, THE ULTIMATE SWORD IS ALREADY FILLED WITH YOUR URGE TO KILL. IT MUST REST IN THE BUDDHA'S HAND TO BE CLEANSED! WITHSTAND ONE MOVE FROM ME, AND IT IS YOURS. THAT'S THE BET.

ALRIGHT!

HOLD ON! I STILL HAVE MY RULES!

IF YOU CANNOT TAKE ONE MOVE FROM ME, THEN YOU MUST STAY HERE WITH MASTER TAOKO FOR TEN YEARS!

HARMONY, HARMONY...

THIS MONK IS ACTUALLY THE LEADER OF THE FORESTALL TEMPLE, AND ALSO THE ELDER DISCIPLE OF MASTER BUSHI.

NAMELESS' POWERS ARE BEYOND ANYONE'S IMAGINATIONS, CLOUD KNOWS THAT HE PROBABLY CAN'T WITHSTAND A MOVE FROM HIM, BUT IF IT'S THE ONLY CHANCE HE HAS TO GET THE SWORD BACK, HE'LL DO IT!

ALRIGHT! MAKE YOUR MOVE!

THERE'S NO RUSH, YOU'RE STILL INJURED, I'LL WAIT UNTIL YOU'VE RECOVERED FROM YOUR INJURIES.

NAMELESS ISN'T PURPOSELY SEPARATING THE ULTIMATE SWORD FROM CLOUD, BUT IS HOPING THAT CLOUD WILL RETURN TO THE RIGHTEOUS PATH, WHICH IS WHY IF HE LOSES, HE'LL HAVE TO STUDY BUDDHISM HERE FOR TEN YEARS.

THERE'S NO TIME, WE'LL FIGHT TOMORROW!

HARMONY! THIS MAY AFFECT YOUR LIFE, YOU MUST THINK CLEARLY!

CLOUD, JIEN-CHEN'S MASTER IS VERY POWERFUL, YOU BETTER NOT BET!

FOOM!

CLOUD!

WITHOUT SAYING ANYTHING, CLOUD RUSHES OUT OF FORESTALL HALL.

MISS CHU CHU, YOU NEED NOT WORRY!

EVEN IF CLOUD LOSES, IT'LL BE FOR THE BETTER THAT HE STAYS HERE FOR TEN YEARS.

YORUO HAS A POINT, BUT CHU CHU STILL FELT WEIRD ABOUT IT ALL. ONLY SHE UNDERSTANDS CLOUD.

...........

MASTER TAOKO, THANK YOU FOR LENDING US YOUR TEMPLE AND MAY I PLEASE ASK YOU TO BE THE WITNESS FOR THIS FIGHT.

YOU'RE WELCOME! I MUST THANK YOU FOR HELPING EVERYONE OUT TO TURN CLOUD AROUND BACK TO THE RIGHTEOUS PATH!

AH YES! IS MASTER BUSHI AROUND? I WOULD LIKE TO GREET HIM!

HMM... HE MUST BE IN "THE CAVE OF WALLS" MEDITATING!

NIGHTTIME

THERE IS PEACE AND QUIET THROUGHOUT THE ENTIRE FORESTALL HALL...

IT IS THE SAME IN THE SAD BUDDHA HALL; PEACEFUL AND QUIET.

A DIM LIGHT IS THE ONLY SOURCE OF LIGHT.

A PERSON SLOWLY ENTERS THE HALL.

TALL, QUIET, WITH HIS LONG CAPE FOLLOWING HIM BY THE BREEZE, IT IS...

CLOUD

HE APPROACHES THE BUDDHA STATUE.

SILENTLY HE WATCHES THE ULTIMATE SWORD IN THE BUDDHA'S PALM.

THEN HE SITS DOWN IN FRONT OF THE BUDDHA AND RESTS.

THIS IS THE FIRST TIME IN HIS LIFE THAT HE HAS SAT IN FRONT OF BUDDHA. THE BUDDHA'S SMILE IS SO PEACEFUL AND SOOTHING... IT'S BEEN SO LONG SINCE SOMEONE HAS SMILED AT HIM LIKE THIS.

BEFORE, HE THOUGHT OF BUDDHA DIFFERENTLY, THINKING THAT THE BUDDHA HAD A FAKE SMILE, AND WAS A FRAUD.

THROUGHOUT HIS LIIFE, BATTLE AFTER BATTLE, CLOUD REMAINED STANDING BECAUSE OF HIS UNDYING HEART. BUT HIS HEART IS GREATLY FATIGUED WITH MANY SCARS! HE NEEDS TO REST!

BUDDHA, I'M ONLY SEEKING REVENGE, I ONLY BELIEVE IN AN EYE FOR AN EYE. I THINK YOU'LL UNDERSTAND!

THERE ARE OTHERS THAT UNDERSTAND CLOUD, SUCH AS THE ULTIMATE SWORD, AND WIND...

PEACE AND QUIET FLOW THROUGH CLOUD'S MIND, AS HE RELAXES INTO HIS OWN WORLD, AS IF HE IS SITTING ON WATER AS CALM AS THE AIR AROUND HIM.

WITH HIS HEART AND MIND QUIETED, HE ENTERS A HIGH LEVEL OF MEDITATION.

HERE, IS A POND SO CALM THAT REFLECTIONS CAN EASILY BE SEEN IN IT... NEXT TO IT LIES A BRUSH, INK, AND PAPER.

THIS IS THE CAVE OF WALLS WITHIN THE FORESTALL TEMPLE. HERE, A MONK HAS BEEN MEDITATING WITHOUT REST OR FOOD FOR THREE DAYS AND THREE NIGHTS.

MASTER BUSHI'S RANK ISN'T LOW AT ALL AMONGST THE OTHERS AT THE FORESTALL TEMPLE. BUT THERE'S SOMETHING BOTHERING HIM, WHICH IS WHY HE'S LOCKED HIMSELF IN THE CAVE OF WALLS FOR SO LONG.

HE FEELS THAT PEOPLE WHO DESERVE PUNISHMENT HAVEN'T BEEN PUNISHED YET, SO HE MUST PUNISH THEM FOR GOD.

THIS IS WHY MASTER BUSHI IS MORE POWERFUL THAN MASTER TAOKO. HOWEVER MASTER TAOKO WAS MADE THE LEADER OF THE FORESTALL TEMPLE.

MASTER BUSHI'S OWN DECISION TO PUNISH OTHERS, IS WHY HE HAS LOCKED HIMSELF IN THE CAVE OF WALLS, WONDERING WHAT HE CAN DO TO HELP THE WORLD.

MEANWHILE... AS CLOUD IS SEEKING PEACE AND QUIET IN THE SAD BUDDHA HALL, OBLIVIOUS TO WHAT IS AROUND HIM...

SUDDENLY, EIGHT SHADOWS FLASH INTO THE SAD BUDDHA HALL.

THE EIGHT SLOWLY FLOAT TO THE GROUND, SHOWING THEY'RE POWER.

CLOUD IS JOLTED OUT OF HIS MEDITATION!

**MASTER TAOKO**

CLOUD, WHAT'RE YOU DOING IN THE SAD BUDDHA HALL IN THE MIDDLE OF THE NIGHT? ARE YOU TRYING TO STEAL THE SWORD?

CLOUD DIDN'T FEEL THAT THERE WAS A NEED TO REPLY... HE ONLY WANTED TO REST. THE SWORD BELONGS TO HIM AND HE'S FIGHTING NAMELESS TOMORROW FOR IT. HE DOESN'T HAVE TO STEAL IT.

THE ULTIMATE SWORD IS ALREADY FILLED WITH YOUR URGE TO KILL! I WILL NOT ALLOW YOU AND THIS SWORD TO KILL ANYMORE!

CLOUD RISES, TIRED OF HEARING THE SAME THING OVER AGAIN..

THE PEACEFUL AND QUIET RESTING PLACE CLOUD WAS LOOKING FOR HAS VANISHED. HE TURNS TO LEAVE.

CLOUD, YOU'RE FULL OF SIN FOR KILLING SO MANY PEOPLE, I MUST DO MY PART AND CALM YOUR HEART AND RID IT OF EVIL!

OLD MONK, DON'T BOTHER WITH MY BUSINESS. IF YOU DO, YOU MAY JUST BRING MISFORTUNE ON YOURSELVES!

BUDDHA BE PRAISED! YOU'RE BECOMING A KILLING MACHINE, I MUST DO WHAT I CAN TO BRING YOU BACK TO THE RIGHTEOUS PATH!

MY BROTHERS! FORM THE "EIGHT LEAFED LOHAN STANCE!"

114

AT MASTER TAOKO'S COMMAND, THE OTHER MONKS FORM A CIRCLE AROUND CLOUD AT EIGHT DIFFERENT PLACES AND TOGETHER CHANT THE WORDS...

AMI TA PHU... AMI TA PHU... AMI TA PHU...

Ami ta phu is a phrase spoken by Buddhist adepts. It means; "Buddha be praised" or "Praise be to Buddha."

THE SO-CALLED EIGHT LEAFED IS SPEAKING OF THE EIGHT LEAVES SURROUNDING THE BUDDHA. ITS POWERS ARE UNLIMITED AND CAN CLEANSE ANY EVIL.

THE EIGHT MONKS TAKE THEIR PLACES AND START THE MEDITATION.

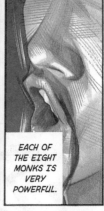

EACH OF THE EIGHT MONKS IS VERY POWERFUL.

WITHIN MOMENTS, CLOUD IS SURROUNDED BY A FORCEFUL MEDITATION AURA.

BOON

YUEK

BOR

LOR

MUT

DOR

SUM

GING!

AS THE EIGHT MASTER MONKS USE THEIR CHI TO SAY EACH WORD LOUD AND CLEAR, MASTER TAOKO FINISHES THE SPELL WITH THE WORD - "GING!"

THIS MEDITATION FORM WAS PASSED DOWN FROM CENTURIES AGO, AS THESE EIGHT MONKS USE THEIR CHI TO FORCE CLOUD TO SURRENDER.

HAH, YOU WANT TO USE YOUR CHI AGAINST MINE AND FORCE ME TO SUBMIT. WHAT KIND OF "PEACEFUL" PLACE IS THIS?

I WILL NOT SURRENDER!

CLOUD BEGINS TO FEEL REST-LESS AS HE'S BEING ATTACKED BY THE EIGHT LEAFED LOHAN STANCE.

MASTER TAOKO USES HIS CHI TO POUND AWAY AT THE DRUM AND DISRUPT CLOUD'S THOUGHTS WHILE HE'S ATTACKED BY THE EIGHT LEAFED LOHAN STANCE.

BUT CLOUD'S HEART HAS NOT GIVEN UP BEFORE. HIS HEART BEATS FASTER AND FASTER!

SUDDENLY, THE NUMEROUS CHAINS OF BEADS FALL ONTO CLOUD, LOCKING AROUND HIS BODY AND BINDING HIS ARMS FROM MOVING EVEN SLIGHTLY!

THE BEADS ARE POWERED BY THE MASTER MONKS' CHI, WHICH IS WHY CLOUD ISN'T ABLE TO BREAK AWAY.

DAMN MONKS!!

CLOUD IS LOCKED DOWN, HE'S REALLY ANGRY NOW!

AT THE CAVE OF WALLS, THE PEACEFUL POND SUDDENLY RIPPLES...

AH!

WHO WOULD'VE THOUGHT EVEN YOU, WHO'S TRAINED FOR S[...] MANY YEARS STI[...] CANNOT HAVE A CLEAR HEART?

MASTER BUSHI DOESN'T EVEN TURN AROUND AND SENDS HIS BEADS FLYING OUT!

BUSHI'S CHI PACKS THE BEADS WITH THOUSANDS OF POUNDS OF PRESSURE -- FLYING AT THE PERSON IN THE DOORWAY.

THE PERSON DOES NOT DODGE THE ATTACK...

THE ATTACK IS STOPPED AS THE BEADS COME TO A HALT.

YOUR SKILLS HAVE IMPROVED A LOT SINCE THE LAST TIME I'VE SEEN YOU. USING YOUR BEADS TO GREET AN ALREADY DEAD FRIEND?!

A MONK HAS NOTHING BUT HIS BEADS. DO YOU EXPECT ME USE CHICKENS AND DUCKS?

"HAS NOTHING..."? I DOUBT THAT... IT LOOKS LIKE YOU STILL HAVE A BURDEN ON YOUR SHOULDERS, WHY ARE YOU FACING THE WALLS AGAIN?

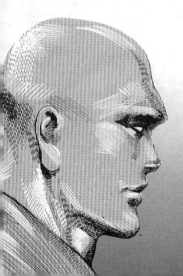

BECAUSE THERE ARE TOO MANY SINFUL PEOPLE IN THE WORLD. KARMA DOESN'T COME FAST ENOUGH, SO I HAVE TO INTERFERE...

THAT'S RIGHT! YOU USED YOUR DEATH AS AN EXCUSE TO RETIRE, WHY COME OUT AND VISIT ME?

I DIDN'T PLAN ON COMING HERE. TODAY I'VE BROUGHT WITH ME AN UNUSUAL PERSON!

WHEN I WAS MEDITATING, I FELT SOMEONE WITH AN EXTREMELY UNUSUAL URGE TO KILL! WHO IS THIS PERSON?

HE'S - CLOUD!

AH, IT'S HIM!

OH, YOU KNOW HIM?

MASTER BUSHI ONCE AGAIN FACES THE WALLS.

WHEN HE WAS THIRTEEN, I HAD BUMPED INTO HIM. WHO WOULD'VE THOUGHT HE WOULD TURN OUT THIS WAY.

HE'S ACTUALLY NOT A BAD PERSON, FULL OF EMOTION. HE IS JUST LOST IN THE TRANCE OF REVENGE, PLACING HIM ON THE PATH OF "DO AS I WILL"!

YOU'RE WRONG, WHEN HE FIRST ONLY WANTED REVENGE, HE WAS ON THE PATH OF "DO AS I WILL", BUT NOW...

I BELIEVE HE'S ON THE PATH OF "NON-RESTORATION."

AS THE WORDS "NON-RESTORATION" ARE SPOKEN, NAMELESS IS SHOCKED. HIS HEART BEATS FASTER AND A THOUSAND WORRIES FLOW THROUGH HIS MIND!

THE BATTLE BETWEEN CLOUD AND NAMELESS... TO THE TWO OF THEM AND TO EVERYONE ACROSS THE LANDS, IT IS EQUALLY IMPORTANT. WHO WILL WIN?

MASTER BUSHI, ASSISTING THE GODS...

NAMELESS, LIMITLESS SWORD STYLE...

CLOUD TURNED FROM THE PATH OF "DO AS I WILL" ONTO THE PATH OF "NON-RESTORATION", WHAT COULD "NON-RESTORATION" MEAN?

**END OF VOLUME 3**

# MA'S NOTES

AS A PROMISE TO THE READERS, I'VE RESUMED MY POST AS EDITOR-IN-CHIEF OF "BLACK LEOPARD," AND SUBSEQUENTLY SUMMONED A MEETING WITH ALL THE CO-WORKERS OF DIFFERENT PRODUCTION DEPARTMENTS TO DISCUSS THE EXISTING PROBLEMS AND SOLUTIONS TO THIS PUBLICATION, HOPING THAT COORDINATION AND COMMON UNDERSTANDING CAN BE MADE POSSIBLE BETWEEN DEPARTMENTS. IN FACT, ALTHOUGH I AM SELDOM DIRECTLY INVOLVED WITH THE EDITING OF "BLACK LEOPARD," I ALWAYS GAVE ADVICE TO IMPROVE THE PRODUCTION. HOWEVER, SOME CO-WORKERS DID NOT FOLLOW MY GUIDELINES STRICTLY, WHICH THEREBY RESULTED IN UNSATISFACTORY PRODUCTION QUALITY. I FELT QUITE DEPRESSED ABOUT THIS OUTCOME.

CONSEQUENTLY, STARTING FROM THE PUBLICATION OF "BLACK LEOPARD," I'VE DETERMINED TO REQUEST EVERY CO-WORKER TO PERFORM THEIR BEST. THEY WILL BE HELD ACCOUNTABLE FOR THEIR JOB FUNCTIONS. I AM INSISTING THE PRODUCTION STAFF NOT TO BE PERFUNCTORY OR SELF-DECEIVED, BUT INSTEAD, TO THINK OF THE READERS FIRST. I TRULY BELIEVE THAT ONLY UNDER THESE GUIDELINES CAN THE BEST WORK BE PRODUCED.

TRACING THE HISTORY OF COMIC DEVELOPMENT IN HONG KONG, WE CAN OBSERVE TWO TYPES OF PRODUCTION MODELS. THE FIRST ONE IS THE "ONE-MAN OPERATION," WHICH IS ALSO A WIDELY ADOPTED MODEL ALL OVER THE WORLD. IT SPECIFICALLY FOCUSES ON AN EDITOR-IN-CHIEF TO SUPERVISE A TEAM OF ASSISTANTS. AS THERE IS ONLY ONE "VOICE OF COMMAND" AND ONE PRODUCTION CONCEPT, ONLY THE PERSONAL STYLE OF THE EDITOR-IN-CHIEF IS REFLECTED. OF COURSE, SUCH A MODEL WOULD TAKE MORE PRODUCTION TIME AND ULTIMATELY INCREASE THE PRODUCTION COST. BUT I IDENTIFY WITH THIS MODEL. STARTING FROM THE PRODUCTION OF "THE CHINESE HERO," TO "STORM RIDERS" AND HENCEFORTH... SO LONG AS I AM THE EDITOR-IN-CHIEF, I WILL ADOPT THIS MANNER OF PRODUCTION.

ANOTHER PRODUCTION MODEL WAS DEVELOPED BY ???? MORE THAN TEN YEARS AGO WHEN THEY WERE ESTABLISHING THEIR COMICS ENTERPRISE. ALL THE WORK AND DETAILS THAT COMPRISE COMICS, SUCH AS THE STORY, WRITING OF SCRIPT, VISUAL COMPOSITION, CHARACTER DESIGN, HAIRSTYLE DESIGN, COSTUMES, WEAPONS AND LOCATION ETC., ARE ALL SHARED BY EXPERTS OF THE RESPECTIVE FIELDS. THE GOOD THING IS, EVERY ARTIST CAN DEMONSTRATE THEIR STRENGTH AND THUS, MAINTAIN THE QUALITY OF THE WORK. SUCH A METHOD IS BENEFICIAL TO THE PUBLICATION OF A WEEKLY MAGAZINE, WHICH FURTHER LEADS TO MARKET EXPANSION. HOWEVER, THE BAD POINT IS, THERE IS A LACKING OF PERSONAL STYLE. IN OTHER WORDS, EACH INDIVIDUAL PRODUCTION DEPARTMENT DOES NOT HAVE TO REPORT TO THE EDITOR-IN-CHIEF, BUT TO THE PRODUCER INSTEAD. IF THE TWO LEADERS DO NOT COMMUNICATE THOROUGHLY WITH EACH OTHER, OR SOME OF THESE DEPARTMENTS HAVE BEEN GLOSSING THINGS OVER, THEN THE PROBLEMS WILL BECOME MORE AND MORE SERIOUS. COMIC BOOK PRODUCTION IS AN ART OF CREATION WHICH REQUIRES ARTISTS TO BE TOTALLY INVOLVED AND RESPONSIBLE. ANY DISTORTION TO THE ARTISTIC ORIGINALITY MIGHT RESULT IN A POOR MEDDLING OF ARTISTIC ELEMENTS AND ULTIMATELY THE LOSS OF PROFESSIONAL AND ARTISTIC INTEGRITY.

"STORM RIDERS" AND "BLACK LEOPARD" HAVE ADOPTED THE ABOVE MENTIONED MODELS RESPECTIVELY. BOTH MODELS HAVE THEIR MERITS AND DEMERITS. I BELIEVE THAT SO LONG AS WE CAN INTEGRATE THEM INTO UNIQUE STYLE, WE CAN COME OUT WITH OUTSTANDING MASTERPIECES WHICH CAN GAIN MARKET PREFERENCE AT THE SAME TIME. THE SUBJECT OF THAT MEETING AS A RESULT, WAS TO LET ALL CO-WORKERS UNDERSTAND THAT THERE WERE DIFFERENT PRODUCTION MODELS APPLYING TO DIFFERENT WORKS. IT IS VITAL TO LEARN HOW TO INTEGRATE THEM TOGETHER.

THE COMICS INDUSTRY IN HONG KONG HAS BEEN CHANGING VIGOROUSLY FOR THE PAST TWO YEARS. RIGHT NOW, UNDER THE FLOURISHING PRODUCTION MODEL OF "DIVISION OF PROFESSIONS," IF THE COMICS PRODUCERS CANNOT IMPROVE THEIR SKILLS, THEY MIGHT BECOME HISTORY ONE DAY. AS A COMIC BOOK ARTIST, I DON'T WANT TO SEE THIS SITUATION WORSEN ANY FURTHER. I WANT TO PROCLAIM TO ALL INVOLVED IN THIS INDUSTRY, TO RECTIFY THEIR BEHAVIOR AND THINK POSITIVELY ON THEIR JOBS, OTHERWISE READERS MIGHT ABANDON US IN THE END. I BELIEVE THAT IF WE CAN WORK SERIOUSLY TOWARDS OUR PROFESSION, THE COMICS INDUSTRY WILL ENJOY A MORE PROSPEROUS FUTURE. THIS IS WHAT I TRULY THINK AND I AM OBLIGED TO SPEAK FROM MY HEART.

FORTUNATELY, AFTER THIS MEETING, THE PRODUCTION OF THE CURRENT "BLACK LEOPARD" HAS BEEN IMPROVING APPARENTLY. EVERYONE IS WALKING TOWARDS MY IDEAL. MY SINCERE ADVICE HAS PROVEN FRUITFUL.

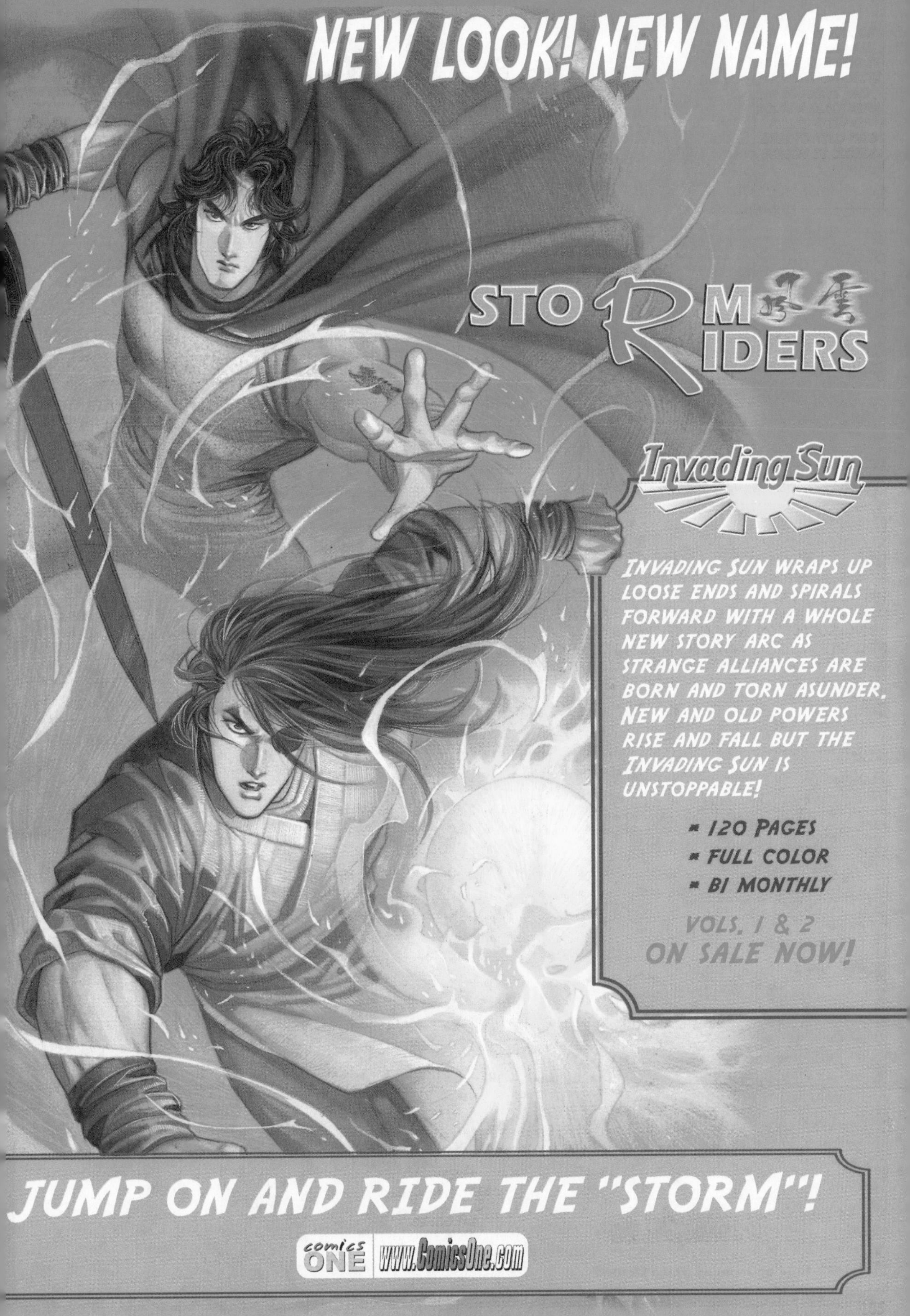
NEW LOOK! NEW NAME!
STORM RIDERS
風雲
Invading Sun
INVADING SUN WRAPS UP LOOSE ENDS AND SPIRALS FORWARD WITH A WHOLE NEW STORY ARC AS STRANGE ALLIANCES ARE BORN AND TORN ASUNDER. NEW AND OLD POWERS RISE AND FALL BUT THE INVADING SUN IS UNSTOPPABLE!
* 120 PAGES
* FULL COLOR
* BI MONTHLY
VOLS. 1 & 2
ON SALE NOW!
JUMP ON AND RIDE THE "STORM"!
comics ONE
www.ComicsOne.com

# STORM 風雲 RIDERS
### by Wing Shing Ma

## A Tale of No Name

A Tale of No Name is the anxiously awaited novel spotlighting Nameless. Here we come to know a very different more brash figure - a change from the humble soft-spoken powerhouse we have grown to love. Learn of young Nameless' upbringing as a youth and how he came to become the venerable character now in the forefront of Storm Riders: Invading Sun!

# STORM 風雲 RIDERS
## Merchandise

## Hero Sword

**Hero Sword:** Master swordsman Nameless of the Storm Riders series, passes this potent yet modest sword to his devoted and skilled student Jien-Chen. The straight sword has always been the weapon of the scholar and ComicsOne's 9-inch Hero Sword is definitely a distinguished way of opening your mail. It ships in a fine wood box perfect for displaying and comes with a jeweled scabbard and a red tassel bound to the hilt. Get yours today!

**Snowy Saber:** One of the most powerful weapons in the entire kung fu world is now available from ComicsOne as one of the most powerful letter openers in the world. Wielded by main character Wind from the popular Storm Riders series, this beautifully crafted 9-inch letter opener is the perfect replica, complete with scabbard and cloth-wrapped hilt. It ships in a fine cherry colored box perfect for displaying. Get yours today!

## Snowy Saber

## Destiny

**Destiny:** The perfect complement to the Snowy Saber and Hero Sword, this curved stainless steel blade is 9 inches long and comes with an ornately detailed scabbard. Store this powerful weapon in its decorative cherry box until the time comes to strike down your enemies or open that ever-menacing utility bill. Get yours today!

## Mini Snowy Saber

**Mini Snowy Saber:** From the pages of Storm Riders comes main character Wind's family blade. Our mini Snowy Saber is the perfect trinket to spruce up your key chain and ward off any would be assailants.

## Flame Kylin Sword

**Flame Kylin Sword:** Young Master Duan-Lang inherits the Flame Kylin after his father's tragic demise. This Duan family heirloom comes in two different flavors. Choose from the jade colored scabbard with a bronze blade or the silver scabbard with matching blade. The Flame Kylin Sword is 5.5 inches long and comes with an elegant red tassel. While the Flame Kylin makes a great letter opener, the sword and scabbard can also double as hairpins.

Please visit our web site for order and weapon information at www.comicsone.com or www.comicsworld.com

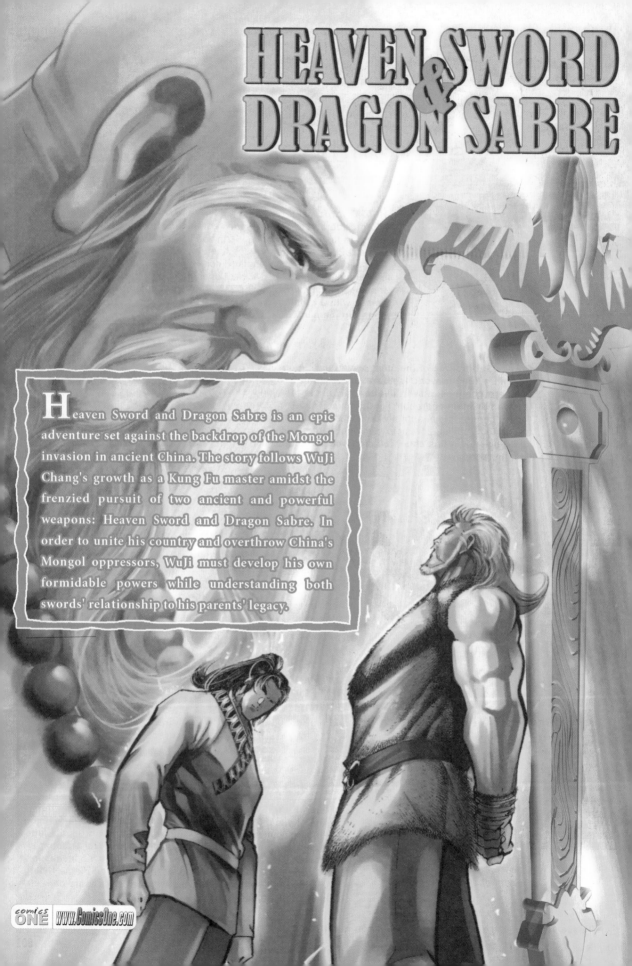

# HEAVEN SWORD & DRAGON SABRE

Heaven Sword and Dragon Sabre is an epic adventure set against the backdrop of the Mongol invasion in ancient China. The story follows WuJi Chang's growth as a Kung Fu master amidst the frenzied pursuit of two ancient and powerful weapons: Heaven Sword and Dragon Sabre. In order to unite his country and overthrow China's Mongol oppressors, WuJi must develop his own formidable powers while understanding both swords' relationship to his parents' legacy.

# BLACK LEOPARD

With the broad and all-encompassing writing style of Storm Riders and the artistic wizardry of Heaven Sword & Dragon Sabre, ComicsOne brings martial arts fans, Black Leopard • Wing Shing Ma's modern day contemporary kung fu epic. Guns blaze, Gangland violence is rampant yet two brothers and their kung fu fighting compatriots show defiance with an iron fist!

英雄

HERO

Wing Shing

Hero illustrated by Wing Shing Ma, is the graphic novel adaptation of Zhang Yimou's breath-taking Oscar nominated feature length martial arts movie. At the height of China's Warring States period, the country was splintered into seven kingdoms: Qin, Zhao, Han, Wei, Yan, Chu and Qi. For years, the separate kingdoms fought ruthlessly for supremacy. This brought decades of death and suffering. The soon-to-be first Emperor of China is on the cusp of conquering the war-torn land, yet three martial arts masters are determined to assassinate him. However one loyal subject stands in their way, ironically in the name of peace for all the land.

# Create Your Own Cosplay Trading Card With Your Image And Text

RAILIENS

White Duelist Utena Tenjou

comics ONE

## COSPLAY TRADING CARDS

**Name:** Stacy Michelle

**Date of Birth:** 7-28-84

**Location:** Central New York

**Likes:** Cats, Halloween, drawing
**Dislikes:** Spiders, ghosts, planes

**Website:**
Lunasea, http://stacy.deviouskitty.com

**Email:** lunaseassiren@yahoo.com

"Be who you are and say how you feel because those who mind don't matter and those who matter don't mind"

www.ComicsOne.com

comics ONE

# 3 Easy Steps

UPLOAD YOUR IMAGE

SELECT A TEMPLATE OF YOUR CHOICE AND CUSTOMIZE IT

YOUR CARDS ARE IN THE MAIL!

# Be Prepared for Your Next Con!
# Available @ ComicsOne.com

comics ONE  www.ComicsOne.com